Black Unity

The Total Solution to
Financial Independence
and Happiness

By Terrance Amen

Published by
T VENTURES
728 Page Street, Suite 2
San Francisco, CA. 94117

ISBN: -10- 0984757236
ISBN: -13- 978-0-9847572-3-7

Table of Contents

ACKNOWLEDGMENTS

I would like to give thanks to the Creator for blessing me with life and a healthy mind to gain knowledge, so that I may continue to grow as a person. I'm thankful for the experiences that helped me to gain wisdom and the understanding to know, I don't know everything. I'd like to thank my moms for saving my life and guiding me in the right direction; she has changed my life forever. I also want to thank my Aunt Sharon for letting me know I wasn't finished writing my book. I also want to thank my friends and acquaintances, who came into my life when I needed them. I'd also like to thank Karen Johnson and the Marcus Books family for helping me get the knowledge and information I needed to complete this book, and also Miss Deeann Mathews for editing and helping me keep as much as I could in the book without compromising her editorial integrity.

DEDICATION

I'd like to dedicate this book to our ancestors who gave their lives in the struggle to unite our people, in order to make a better life for us here and all over the world. I'd also like to dedicate this book to those who live and work today to help us come together in order to reach our full potential and be the best we can be. Finally, I'd like to dedicate this book to the millions of brothers and sisters who supported our many leaders over the years and have proved that when we come together, there's nothing we can't do.

INTRODUCTION

We are achieving financial independence and happiness in our community; the problem is that only a small percentage of us are achieving this compared to the masses of our people. How do we turn this around so the masses benefit as well? It's simple: through unity.

But why aren't we united – like so many other groups – if it will benefit the majority of us? We have the intelligence, money, and resources. By the time you finish this book, you will have a simple, no-excuse plan on how to bring back one hundred billion dollars and more that we spend every year with other groups, but not ourselves. This will also allow us to create the jobs and services that will continue to help us unify our resources in order to create the financial independence and happiness we deserve. This will be better for us than waiting for someone else to give us jobs that continue to keep us dependent on others and deny us the services that help bring us together.

This is not just a book; this is a blueprint to our success in every area of our lives, including financial, business, health, family, education, politics, and more, now and in the future. You will also know the reason why we don't have a plan like this in place now and why it has been over seventy years since this was last attempted.

There are two main parts to this book: the problems and the solutions. I'd like to start on a positive note, talking about the solutions and the amazing effects they will have on our lives if we just utilize a fraction of what we already spend. Some of you may already know what the problems are and would rather focus more on the solutions. Then there are some of you who may not be convinced we even have a problem.

You may not like the language I use in the part I have titled "The Problem" because what I refer to may not pertain to you. But you will know if it does, based on what you do (or choose not to do) by the time you finish that part. I apologize if I offend you, for that is not my purpose. My purpose is to make you intensely aware of our problems, (which have been with us since our ancestors first became free in this country) and how to fix those problems. I consider us family, and you know family can be your worst critic.

Please look at this as a family member offering tough love. I write these words to you in the hope that we can unite by finding common ground. If you are young, middle-aged, senior, wealthy, poor, or anywhere in between, there's something for you in these pages that you can connect with and will speak to your needs. That's why my title is *The Total Solution to Financial Independence and Happiness*. My goal is to give you as many reasons and positive incentives possible to see the need to commit to supporting ways that will build unity rather than division, to showing love and respect, to being more inclusive rather than exclusive, and to help all of us become the best that we can be physically, mentally, spiritually, and financially as a united people.

We have a serious problem with not uniting and working together in order to create the opportunities that most other groups enjoy. Instead of having our hands out and complaining about the crumbs we continue to accept, we should be taking advantage of the fortunes we give away every day, fortunes that keep every other group wealthy and happy, while we continue to suffer and complain. We can finally flip the script and reverse all the negative things that have kept us from being a successful united community, just by doing something we've done in the past. It is possible for us to go from victims to over-achievers. We've done it before; that's how we got this far. Now it's time to unite and move from victimhood to achievement as a community. It's up to us to change our circumstances.

You may not agree with everything you read in these pages. It is my hope that you do agree with the most important message of the book: in order for us to reach our full potential, we must unite and start working together on a national and global level. This is not the be-all and end-all, but a great start. In these pages is a plan that begins the solution to the most important issues we face in our lives as a people. This plan covers all the major issues you face in your life everyday. That's a bold statement to make, but I'll let you be the judge.

We are our own worst enemy now. We can no longer keep blaming the white man for our problems. It's time to look in the mirror to see who's really to blame now. Yes, the white man of the past created the problems, and racism is alive and well today. That's why no matter how successful or unsuccessful an individual may be, we are all in the same boat. But today, we as a people have become our biggest obstacle to being happy and prosperous by the way we're portrayed and by our own actions.

The great news is that you can also be the solution to our problems; our success or failure in life lies in our own hands. If you read this book to the end, you'll see the book contains the total solution to our coming together to reap the full benefits of what we have to offer this country and the world. None of this is new except for my focus on what I believe is the real issue that keeps us as a people from being the best we can be. This book is an updated version of what our great leaders and thinkers have been trying to do since we were brought here in chains to this country.

It will take a collective effort of the most dedicated people (of which there are many) to implement this plan. These people are the ones you don't hear about. They are the ones doing what needs to be done every day without looking for headlines, until they finally get recognized for all their years of hard work. We have what we need among our own people; all we need is to pull together.

Do you ever ask yourself how it is that different groups of people who come to this country become successful after living here such a short period of time, when we as a people continue to struggle? Some say newer immigrant groups get help from the government, and that may be true. But I believe the real answer is that the newcomers are united, work together, support one another, network, speak their own language, and keep their culture intact. They know exactly who they are and where they came from, and are proud of it.

What makes us different? We haven't really addressed the differences because we have often been distracted from them. If enough people talk about and take action on the real problems, rather than the superficial ones, we would finally have a chance to start solving these problems. So now, let's see what we could create if we unite and work together to become a happy and financially independent people.

THE SOLUTION

The Organization

What if we created a Black membership organization, whose sole purpose is to reprogram, reorganize, and uplift the Black community in every area of life, for the betterment of all our people? In this organization, we would create a variety of programs and incentives to get us to work together and give ourselves as many reasons as possible to support the organization and each other. All programs, departments, and services in the organization will be run by experienced professionals in their chosen fields. The organization would also be an umbrella which would cover other organizations that have expertise in the many areas listed in this section, finding the best to support and expand so not to be redundant in any area.

The organization would allow you to save on everyday products and services you buy and use. The difference between the wholesale price and the retail price of products and services would help build a financial base for the organization, and this would be supplemented by an annual membership fee. This will allow the organization to grow and circulate money within the community by buying products and services from Black businesses, and eventually Black producers of products and services. This financial base is essential to achieving self-sufficiency; without self-sufficiency, little else can be accomplished. In addition, the organization's only focus will be to find ways to help make the lives of Black people better.

The value you will receive from the organization will be many times greater than what you contribute.

Just harnessing our buying power alone would make the organization worth supporting. Let's start capitalizing on the billions we spend with other groups who don't spend their hard-earned money in our community. Think about all the products and services you use; think about all the ones you either have to go out of your neighborhood to get, or you have to give your money to someone who doesn't give back to your community. The organization would solve this problem; can you imagine all the savings you would receive by buying together with your people as a group?

This kind of buying is called discount volume buying. With *discount volume buying*, our people would save on almost anything you can think of, and in this way part of that nearly $1 trillion we give away every year would stay in our communities (yes, we as a people are getting close to a trillion dollars of disposable income, the money we have to spend after paying our taxes). This is how other groups of people have become successful in a short period of time. We need to use our collective buying power; as other groups have shown, it pays to work together. This is the only way we will be successful as a people.

Think about this: if we were a nation by ourselves, we would be wealthier than many of the countries you've heard about. That's how much money we have to spend, and united, that's how money and power we would have. I'm talking about creating a nation within a nation, which is kind of what we already have, but we're just not the ones benefiting from it. We can change this and reap the full benefits of being a united people. We're talking about the redistribution of wealth here – after all, aren't you tired of seeing other people come into your neighborhood, taking your hard-earned money, and then leaving to support their communities? I know I am.

Instead, in the organization, we could have a directory of Black businesses in each city we would support, based on those who are members, and what non-members are giving back – or not giving back – to the community. The directory will cover different categories of products and services. If we utilize just a fraction of these opportunities by keeping the money in our community, we'll do very well.

How about having your taxes done by members of the organization who are qualified tax preparers and accountants, who will make sure you're paying the least amount of taxes as possible, represent you if you ever get audited, and give back to you by providing you with discounts? Tax software could be created as well, for those who would rather do their own taxes. All the money would stay in the community, instead of going to H&R Block and other similar companies.

How about having credit unions for savings and loans, where you don't have to worry about not getting a loan based on someone looking down at you because of the color of your skin, or your social status?

There are Black associations in every field of expertise. Imagine having access (at a discount) to doctors and lawyers dedicated to the welfare of your community!

How about having our own teachers and our own schools, where our children's gifts can be nurtured instead of discouraged. We ourselves can teach our own children the information and skills they need to be successful in every area of their life?

How about buying groceries and products that are produced and distributed by organization members who look like you and give back to your community? How about supporting Black farmers to produce our own food? As it is now, Black farmers are losing their farms at an incredible rate (because of racist attitudes by government workers, whose job it was to give those loans the Black farmers were qualified to receive. Instead of our farmers having to beg from the government, we could have our own stores to carry their produce, and have our own financial institutions help them. These farmers need our help, and we can use theirs, in order to grow and create new businesses. Glory Foods and some Black hair care products are examples of this.

The organization will obtain buildings that will be accessible to all of our communities. This real estate investment will provide us places to have our stores, our credit unions, our professional services, our schools, and our places to reeducate ourselves to be the best we can be financially, physically, mentally, and spiritually.

What about reparations? Do you think we will ever get our forty acres and a mule, which by now would be equivalent to owning this country, since it was our ancestors' labor that created the wealth? I don't think so. Instead of shouting, fighting, suing, and wasting time and money for something we will never get to the degree we deserve, let's take what we're owed by creating opportunities that will get other groups to buy from us. Another way is by doing something we've done in the past.

Take the Montgomery Bus Boycott as an example. The main reason the boycott started was because Black people were fed up with paying their hard-earned money only to be told to give up their seat when a white person didn't have one. So they got together to boycott the bus system, after Miss Rosa Parks wouldn't give up her seat. This almost bankrupted the bus company. We used the power of our wealth by withholding it from the bus system until it served us; that's how we got to sit wherever we wanted on the bus.

We succeeded in the boycott not only because we marched and protested, but because we united and helped each other. We drove those who didn't have cars to the places they needed to go. Those of us who were not in the region sent donations – brothers and sisters all across the country supported and believed in what was happening. We remained unified around this issue until the Supreme Court made the ruling that finally integrated the public bus system in the South.

So I say again, how do we get reparations? We can take what is rightfully ours simply by creating businesses and services that allows other groups to buy from us while redirecting how we spend the money we already use on products and services. There's a saying: "Money talks and the rest walks." Money is power, and when you have it or take it away, you get the respect you deserve. We have a choice where to spend our money. So why continue to give your money to every group but your people? The organization would make it possible for you to work collectively with other Black people to use your dollars to build up your own community.

The organization would also offer education; we need to reprogram ourselves, to shake off the negative effects of what's been called the slave mind, which will be detailed later in this book. Among its many services, the organization would also offer classes for both adults and young people on vital subjects including nutrition, exercise, self defense, general education, language, finances, and meditation. Members would also be able to access the organization's website to get the information they need as well (after all, we do live in and need to be equipped for the technology age).

Of course, not everyone who joins the organization will fully practice all the rules and policies of the organization at first. Some members will be totally committed to the organization and its tenets because these members will understand the importance of complete unification. Others will become members just to save money and take advantage of the opportunities to get loans, higher interest rates, or just to be part of something positive, and worthwhile. But less-committed members will become more involved when they see the success fully committed members achieve.

There will be different levels of organization membership based on commitment: general, associate, and leader. General members will be defined as those interested in supporting the organization to take advantage of the commercial opportunities offered. Associate members will be defined as those willing to go further to learn more about and participate in the educational and cultural opportunities the organization has to offer and participate in them. Leader members will be defined as those fully committed to all aspects of the organization and are able to represent the organization to the general public. This group will lead the organization and help to produce future leaders for the organization and our people.

The organization will have the right to kick out members who don't follow the minimal rules of being in the organization. For example, drinking or smoking will not be permitted in any of the organization's buildings. Members will also be asked to confine those activities to the comfort and privacy of their own homes, and not engage in drinking or smoking in the street or in bars where potential misbehavior can be seen by the world at large. We are trying to change the perception of how people look at us, and more importantly, how we look at ourselves.

In addition, any organization that tried to unite our people in the past was infiltrated by people whose agenda was not uniting our people. There will be traitors who look like us; the organization will maintain a watchful stance. As a protective measure, this organization will be set up so that it doesn't need a supreme leader or a figurehead. It must be able to stand on its own merits, regardless of who is in charge of running the organization.

The organization will also establish a protection group of volunteers, to help protect our communities from the inside and out.

Why is such an organization necessary? And why haven't we created it already? We need to look at why we have so often chosen to support other groups instead of our own; this is an essential part of the reeducation program we must complete in order to unite and achieve the success that is possible for us, and much of the rest of the book will begin this process.

RE-EDUCATION

Until we acknowledge and solve the psychological effects of slavery and colonialism, we will never reach our full potential as a people. So how do we change the negative effects of slavery? The easy answer is to just do the opposite of what we're doing now, by creating, manufacturing, supporting and buying Black products and services. Unfortunately it's not that easy. We have literally been programmed NOT to succeed, and this can only be overcome through our total re-education.

When Europeans took our ancestors from Africa, our Motherland, they took the cream of the crop, the ones most likely to succeed. They didn't take the old or the sick; the Europeans took our warriors, farmers, scientists and leaders. This left the peoples remaining in Africa easier to conquer and exploit, while the best and the brightest were enslaved to use their talent to enrich Europeans in Europe and in the Americas.

Our ancestors were strong enough to survive the horrific voyage called the Middle Passage; they survived the inhuman treatment and conditions that killed half or more of the Africans who went through it. But the Europeans were smart enough to know they needed to create a system to control such a strong people, and they began a process of negative programming that divides us to this day. Our ancestors were programmed not to trust one another, or work together except in working for the slave master. They were taught to judge each other based on skin color and to only look out for the individual, and not the community. This was so well taught that some slaves would tell the slave master of other slaves' plans to escape, in order to be in the master's favor.

Unfortunately, a lot of us still act out this programming today, without being aware of it. We still talk about the differences in our skin color. A light-skinned woman (sometimes called "redbone") is presumed to look better than a dark-skinned woman; straight hair is supposed to be better than curly hair. We also have not had an organization of at least a million members that covered our financial, health, social, political, educational, and cultural issues. The last time we had an organization with this many members was in the early 1900s, when the United Negro Improvement Organization (UNIA) was founded by Marcus Garvey.

Every successful organization we had was brought down with the help of someone who was Black. We do have large members in religious organizations, but unfortunately our religious organizations are divided as well, and in the past, many religious organizations were also used to keep us under control.

The horrible habits of distrust toward one another, of colorism, of lack of concern about the Black community as a whole, will take time to break, but we can break those habits if we focus on breaking them and creating better ones. After all, we break bad habits and create good ones everyday. We lose weight, we stop smoking, and we start exercising and eating right when we see these things are essential to our survival. We can also break the habits of not trusting and working with one another, do the work together that is necessary for our survival, and reap the benefits of our labor by becoming happy and prosperous.

A panel of top psychologists in the field of re-education and reprogramming can be put together within the organization, to figure out the best and fastest way to reprogram our minds so we can finally end the negative effects of slavery. It is important for us to include techniques that access the power of the subconscious mind to help us do what we need to do. It is also important to study the effects on children and adults watching programs portraying people who don't look like them or have the same experiences they do. Once the results are found, we need to find ways to counteract those effects.

How about some practical good habits we can start? An easy way to create good habits is to set up a plan that helps us do it automatically, so we don't even have to think about it. A financial habit would be direct deposit. Direct deposit is a simple way to allow us to save money without having to think about it. A cultural habit would be listening to music that reminds you of what you should do as a Black person, like McFadden and Whitehead's song, "Ain't No Stopping Us Now."

(Speaking of music, a cultural habit we need to break is watching videos and listening to music that glorifies sex and disrespects women. Our refusal to patronize such music will let artists know they need to make more music that is positive and inspiring. An example of this was the positive music of Tupac Shakur, may he rest in peace. On the one hand, he glorified the thug life, on the other, he preached and rapped about positive and unifying themes, including love and respect of mothers in "Dear Mama," and of not giving up in "Keep Ya Head Up.")

If you're religious, you can add uniting our people to your prayer; if you're not, you can chant or meditate. An artistic habit would be to create posters with positive affirmations, so you will see these affirmations, hear them, say them, and do them. The key is to do it every day at the same time. In the back of the book you will find Ten Guidelines of Black Unity that will give you a place to start your affirmations. These ten guidelines are not new; they are just reminders to help us remember what it takes to take care of you, your family, and your community first, before you take care of someone else who is definitely not looking out for you.

These guidelines will not only help to unite us, but help us grow as a people in all aspects of our lives. By reciting these and applying the guidelines everyday you will begin to change your attitude, and instead of thinking about it, you'll be living it. The key is to reprogram ourselves in order to take advantage of the opportunities to work together.

Let's consider the opportunities that exist for us in supporting Black businesses. There are Black businesses out there, but we have been programmed to not support them, and some Black business owners have been programmed to think their own people are not worthy of high-quality products and services. We all know stories of Black business people who are late, have a bad attitude, offer inferior products and services; our bad programming kicks in when we keep telling those stories and stop looking for Black businesses that can provide the quality of product and service that we want.

Our bad programming also kicks in when we fail to consider that we can create the businesses we need. All of this can change for the better when we start to program ourselves to love, respect, support, and treat each other like family, not the enemy.

There are Black businesses out there, but not nearly enough to support our community, so there are plenty of opportunities out there. The organization will help to identify and foster Black business activity in all aspects, through its membership and purchasing power.

One large business opportunity that can help us reeducate ourselves is in the area of media. Our writers and producers can create TV and online video programs that educate, motivate, and support our young children and adults. With the power of the Internet, this can be done easily and at little cost. Black History can be showcased in this way, a way that is both educational and entertaining.

Another way to reprogram ourselves is to focus more on education and related fields instead of sports and entertainment. That leads to the next subject, of properly educating our children and some adults by letting them know it is okay to love education and be the best you can be. It's time to break this pattern of our youth thinking it's not cool to be educated. It's a shame our young brothers and sisters have to rot in jail because they don't know how to use their minds and imaginations in order to create the life they want without using illegal means.

We have to stop sending our children into the world unprepared, while expecting them to be successful. If we are going to reprogram ourselves as a people, we must address this issue. In some cities the high school dropout rate is over fifty percent. There are students graduating who can barely read. Teachers aren't the only ones to be blamed for this. The public education system is failing our children, and so are we as parents, family members, teachers, and so-called leaders of the community – we will continue to fail unless we take responsibility back into our own hands.

EDUCATION

As part of its educational programs, the organization will help give students the skills they need to be successful and ready to be the best they can be. Members who will teach will do this in the organization's buildings, churches, online, or all of the above until we have our own centers and schools. African history will be the foundation upon which our children (and some adults who have been denied the knowledge) can gain pride and build confidence on. This is necessary because so little of the history and contributions of Africans and African Americans are talked about in public school, except in February, which is the only month designated in the mainstream of this country as "Black History Month." And when February comes, the schools rarely focus on anything other than slavery and the civil rights period. But the history of African peoples is far too long and great to be limited to one month; we ourselves must make up the difference for our young people and all others in our community who want to learn. The organization will provide structure and space for this learning to occur.

What subjects from Black history would education fostered by the organization cover? Let's consider the needs of our youngest children. They need to know, from a very early age, that Kemet (Egypt) was once the educational center of the world – that their ancestors were the original teachers of the knowledge used by all civilizations since. Our young people need to know about our holocaust, how millions of our people died in Africa, on slave ships, and here in America. No one will ever tell our story better than the people whose ancestors went through it and what really happened. No one will ever tell it better than we can tell it for ourselves. Our young people need to know the major contributions Africans contributed not only here in the United States, but to the world down through its history. In this way, the learning of standard subjects – reading, writing, reasoning, mathematics, and science – will be put in a context that helps our young people, and all of us, succeed.

The organization's educational provisions will also include teaching our children how to use their time wisely. One of the reasons our children get into trouble is because they have too much idle time on their hands with no direction or guidance, and part of this has to do with how we have allowed the so-called "generation gap" to shut down our children's respect and service to our elders.

In the days of our grandparents and great-grandparents, respect for elders was the norm. We must educate our children to again show that respect, and serve their elders by assisting them in day-to-day tasks such as grocery shopping and housework. This will also help our children learn to respect the community as a whole, and to serve by doing community service and volunteer work, cleaning the sidewalks in their neighborhoods, and other productive tasks. These productive, community-oriented activities teach our children traditions, values, and skills that will help them become better students, leaders, artists, and whatever else they may dream to be.

The organization's educational provisions would also include introducing students (young and old) to the major languages of Africa. This will help us develop a stronger cultural identity, and help us connect with some of our brothers and sisters in Africa. For example, millions of our people celebrate Kwanzaa every year, and the terms associated with Kwanzaa are in Swahili. So we already have some familiarity with Swahili; the next step is to learn Swahili and other major African languages, and use those languages in communicating and collaborating with our brothers and sisters in Africa.

The orientation of education within the organization will be to encourage and support our children in using their talents and pursuing their dreams, instead of discouraging them by telling them what they can't do. An education based on discouragement makes children look outside the home and community for support and encouragement – and the streets and media are the first place they look, streets and media that reinforce the limiting idea that the only ways to succeed are to become a rapper, singer, drug dealer, or athlete.

Our children need to know there are more opportunities out there than what they see in mass media and on the corner; it's up to parents, teachers, community, and community leaders to let our children know the many career options they have to choose from. The organization will assist through its educational outlook and programs.

Technology will be a major tool; software and the Internet can be used to help students of all ages, as well as their parents, with teaching and learning at home. This is particularly important because the organization will not immediately have buildings and centers everywhere; in the meantime, members will still be able to get their children what they need to excel in their classes at school.

Many of the organization's early educational pro- grams will be preliminary to having our own schools. This is especially necessary because we have so many of our children growing up in foster care, group homes, and daycare centers; we as a community have to have control of the rules and formats so we can encourage our chil- dren's positive growth. Schools on this order have suc- cessfully been created before.

One well-known founder of such a school is Miss Marva Collins. She got fed up with the Chicago school system and started Westside Preparatory School. Through her teaching methods she was able to raise the test scores of her students who were considered low-achieving and outcast at other schools, while teaching these students life skills as well. Miss Collins was nationally recog- nized for this achievement and won many awards for her accomplishments. Providence St. Mel is another school in Chicago that has had an outstanding record of excel- lence for over thirty years. Another excellent program is the Harlem Children's Zone, which has been showcased on *60 Minutes* and CNN.

Having our own schools from pre-kindergarten to middle school is a major step in setting our children on the path to success. Instead of our children being the worst in class, they would become the best. We could have our top athletes start to go back to Black universi- ties and bring championships back to our schools. These athletes would also get a better education, and our col- leges would receive some of those millions of media dollars that white schools receive from having our athletes play.

Perhaps a "super team" could be created, where the top players go to one major Black college. This would give the school, conference, and community much-needed exposure and money. More schools can be added to strengthen the conference, and we can continue to build from there.

Here's an example of how funneling our athletes through our own schools can change a situation that is deteriorating: have you noticed that there are fewer and fewer Black baseball players? Have you noticed that players that look like us are increasingly being recruited in Latin America? If we had our own schools, we could work with Black baseball players who are already involved in bringing baseball back to our communities across the country. Black colleges could also play a role in this area, and this could produce an additional stream of income for them.

Education offered by the organization, before and after we have set up our own schools, must also help those who've been incarcerated. Some of our smartest and brightest are already in jail, and programs need to be set up to help reeducate them while they're inside and out. This is why it is also so important to create and support Black businesses, which are the most likely to create jobs for those coming out of prison, so those that do come out don't go back to their old ways and repeat the cycle of going in and out of jail.

The United Negro College Fund raises roughly 130 million dollars a year for our students' education. That's it and that's all. This is disgraceful and unacceptable, considering the hundreds of billions of dollars of disposable income we waste every year on things that have little to no value. By utilizing and supporting the organization, we could raise billions of dollars to educate our children.

Even though the cost of education continues to go up, there's no reason why our children should have to struggle with tuition in order to go to college. We have the money, so what are we teaching our children about priorities when we tell them that in order to get a good job you have to have a good education, but when it's time to go to college, we don't have the money to send them to the best schools? Our young people end up going in debt, having to end their education in community college, or both. It is important to start preparing for our children's education early; by doing so, the cost will be less overall. We can do this simply by redirecting the way we spend our money and starting their college funds when they are born. One way to make sure we have that money, collectively, is to use our collective buying power through the organization.

The organization will also set up scholarships for students who would be willing to study in the professions we need in our communities. Our young people certainly need to be prepared for the emergence of green technology jobs and associated opportunities, and also need to think about becoming entrepreneurs instead of always working for someone else. The organization will also provide access to programs and tests that can guide our young people to discover what they're most interested or gifted in.

Instead of having our children be raised by other people who don't look like us, we also can create our own day care centers and group homes for troubled teens to give them the education, support and love they deserve, and to let them know we haven't abandoned them.

Many of the people that care for and educate our children now work only because of the money they hope to make, not whether the children that they are caring for are given the love and attention they deserve. When we return to caring for our own children, we can teach them values and life skills so they will be prepared for life, instead of allowing other people to just look at them as a meal ticket and a way to make money. This could also be a way to prevent these young people in need from becoming another statistic in the criminal system, and also a way to generate income in our community.

All the re-educational and educational steps described in this book are needed on a united, organized, and national level. Specific programs can strategically be based on criteria that may include getting the maximum results with minimum cost in the shortest period of time, or reaching the maximum amount of students. A national survey can be taken by a panel of educators with proven results in the success of our students, to determine which programs to implement. There really is no secret to what works; I've given examples of our educators succeeding in educating our children. We just need to implement what works for us on a national, unified level, and working through the organization will help us do that.

FAMILY

The Black family is not what it used to be. Everybody loves to use our saying, "it takes a village to raise a child." The saying describes how we raised our children by using our extended family and neighbors to watch our children when we couldn't. Now, daycare centers, strangers, TV and the Internet are taking care of our children. What happened?

Part of the reason is that we moved away from each other; many of us no longer have the strong, extended families to help us. And, we don't have relationships with our neighbors like we used to; we live in mixed neighborhoods more often now, and the value systems are often different. Last but not least, the two-parent family has become or is becoming the exception rather than the rule. That's a basic issue; let's start there.

As you may already know, there is a major problem between Black men and women when it comes to relationships. Our identities, roles, morals, and values have changed, mainly because of economics, the separation of the extended family, and society's values. The CNN special, *Black in America 2*, goes into details about these different reasons. For one, we've lost our African traditions that gave us order and strong values, and are instead following Eurocentric traditions and values, which have proven less stable. In addition, according to the 2007 US Census, 59 percent of the Black population in this country is either divorced or has never been married (not counting the other 4 percent of Black people that have separated from their mates). Slavery also played a major role in the dysfunction of our relationships by separating the family, which broke the bonds of marriage and parenthood.

I think the welfare system is another major problem; in some ways, it was one of the worst programs ever offered to us. It made us dependent on the government rather than independent, relying on ourselves, largely because the system offered few incentives for us to ever get off of it. Most of us, because of our human nature, will always take what we believe to be the easier path; welfare is set up to make it easy for us to remain on the path of least resistance, even though that path is not taking us to the betterment of our total situation as a people.

More critically, the welfare system has helped to exclude fathers from their households. To receive welfare, a family cannot have the father stay in the household, and the benefits are often more than a working father can earn. So, a father trying to uphold his responsibilities suddenly becomes a source of hardship for the whole family. This poses a challenge and causes heated discussions for the two parents; the father has to deal with knowing he may not be able to make enough to take care of his family, and the mother has to deal with knowing that she could receive more from welfare than the father can bring in. Fathers in this situation often leave because of their wounded pride and frustration. We don't have to agree with those decisions, but we need to understand the cycle.

When fathers leave, that leaves the mother to have to take over the role of breadwinner and father figure as best she can. (A great example of the welfare system and how it helps to keep fathers or male figures away is the movie *Claudine,* in which the mother had to represent the bread winner and the father figure).

As a consequence, some women began to think it was okay to have sex out of wedlock and have children because they had a safety net to fall back on if the relationship didn't work out. Now imagine generations of young girls growing up thinking they really don't need a man to support them and help raise their children. To them, men primarily become sex objects and not the husbands, protectors, providers, and fathers they once were. The trouble is that these same ideas also produce generations of young boys growing up thinking their only responsibility is to produce children, while the woman does everything else.

Many successful women, because of their earning power, seem to be even more intent on thinking they don't need a man except for sex. This type of attitude denies men the respect many of them need to try to become more than just a sex object. Because many of these same men don't have examples of how to be a father and supporter, the cycle of women raising boys continues. The traditional roles have changed, and not just in the Black community. But we are the ones suffering the most from the change.

To reverse this, we must go back to having strong family values and the traditions we used to have, when there was no welfare and we could only rely on ourselves and our communities. We need programs to help us understand the roles men and women should have. Churches can play a major role by utilizing the institutions they already have in place; the organization also will be supporting rites of passage programs that will be created across the country.

Now I'm not talking about keeping the woman home to just cook, clean, and raise children, although I think this could be an option for a lot of women who are tired of doing it all. What I'm talking about is getting back to a balance of roles and responsibilities again, rather than the woman doing everything. Since slavery, Black women have had to be the backbone of the Black race because of the extraordinary efforts to weaken and destroy Black men. But now it is time for the Black man to take his rightful place as the head of the household. What I'm talking about is encouraging the man to become the husband, supporter, protector, and father figure he was meant to be, relieving the woman of having to fulfill both adult roles in the family.

There are a lot of opportunities for women to make more money than men these days, partially because of racism, and partially because more women are going to college than men, as you can see in *Black in America 2* from CNN that I've already referred to. Still, there are a lot of good men out there who don't make a lot of money but are capable of being good husbands and fathers for their children. I'm talking about the women who make more money than their men, but the men are still good men. But some of these women would rather have status than a good husband and father figure. Unfortunately, everything financially is not always going to be equal – at least, not yet. The organization will also help families save money through their discount programs from buying together.

If you look at the different communities like the African, Asian, Middle Eastern, and South American communities, their family values are intact. They know the roles men and women should have, and there seem to be fewer problems in their lives and communities. Their children are more prepared for adulthood and have examples of what a successful family looks like. When people from different countries keep their cultural and family values, there are fewer problems because they know their roles and it works for them. Are they perfect? Of course not. But often, when these groups change their family values to fit this society's so-called norm, things do not always change for the better.

In a sense, it is best to maintain traditional family values and not adopt the "do whatever you want" lifestyle that is the norm for families today. This lifestyle has been proven to not work, considering that now almost half the marriages today end in divorce. Men and women are producing babies out of wedlock as never before, and children are having sex before they know anything about their bodies.

We must hold ourselves accountable for the way we raise our children. It takes unconditional love to raise a child; sacrifice has to be the norm and not the exception. If we are going to have children, we must take full responsibility for them, and make sure they are fully equipped and prepared to be successful in life. We need to provide them with education, good values, respect, patience, and all the other attributes needed to be a successful, well-rounded person. These are the qualities we so often haven't passed down to our children; we've filled the gap with material things that have no long-term worth, and reinforced a skewed, selfish value system.

A great movie that emphasizes unconditional love and the sacrifices you have to make is the movie *Gifted Hands*, the incredible true story of the world-renowned surgeon Dr. Benjamin Carson, and his brother Curtis, who is an engineer. The book is also a great example to teach young and old people about striving for excellence. Another great movie is *The Pursuit of Happyness*. If you haven't seen these movies already, you really need to see them. I think they are great examples of parents' unconditional love for their children. These movies also show the horrible trials and tribulations many have to go through in growing up with a single parent, getting a job, and working for people who don't look like or care much for us.

Men and women need to realize how important it is to raise a child, and the importance of having both parents in the household. Children are not only our future, but they are gifts and blessings that we should cherish and guide, in order to help them reach their full potential. The cycle of fathers abandoning their children is a horrible consequence of disunity and lost values and must be stopped.

For a boy not to have his father creates an unbalanced adult who really doesn't have the knowledge of how to be a complete man. A mother can teach all the qualities it takes to be a man, but only a man can be that example for the child to see. Young men who crave the father figure will seek it anywhere they can get it. These young men may not always get the best examples, which is why they end up continuing the cycle of abandoning their children. A father is also very important for the daughter, so she can see an example of how a man is supposed to treat her through his relationship with her mother. Without this, she has no idea of how to choose a good man; thus, the cycle of women choosing men for all the wrong reasons continues.

This is why re-educating and re-programming is so important if our community is to be successful. The negative cycles can end with a commitment to accepting the fact that things need to change and a willingness to be that change, utilizing tools that are already out there, and also made available by the organization to help transform the Black man and woman. Women need to do the same, in understanding that choosing a man is a very important step in your happiness and your family's happiness.

The organization will be providing rites of passage programs for children and adults to help men and women know who they are, what is expected of them, and how to choose the right kind of mate, and also will be providing advisers so that men and women can learn to have more fruitful and successful relationships.

Sex should not be the main criteria in having a successful relationship. Sex is a physical and emotional act that gives you pleasure for a short period of time. When the sex is over, we still have to deal with each other on a mental level. We spend more time on the mental plane then the physical, so it makes more sense to get to know a person on a mental level before ever thinking about the physical level. In today's society, we do the opposite, which is probably why our relationships don't last.

We have to ask ourselves what we want: a purely physical relationship, or a mental one? You do have a choice. A purely physical relationship is simply that, but a mental relationship includes the total package. A woman's body is sacred and should only be given to the man who has made a commitment to love, respect, and protect her for the rest of her life. This means marriage, which has been proven to work. The organization will put together panels of people who have successful marriages; people on the panels will be able to teach and advise those who want to be married on what it takes to be successful.

Without the total commitment of marriage, how are you going to know if a man or woman really loves you? It takes unconditional love between a man and woman to have a successful marriage, and that is also the basis for successful child-rearing. Both partners in a romantic relationship should be committed to each other for at least six months to get to know each other before marriage is even thought about.

For people who are already in relationships that have gone bad: Brothers, try to reconnect and make amends with your wives, women, and children. It's never too late to do the right thing. You might be able to work it out with a new attitude, and the tools to make your families life better. If you're not accepted, at least you tried, but always stay in touch in case they need you. The organization will help by providing group support in order to help bring communication back into couples' lives.

Sisters, be more forgiving – if not for your own sake, then for your children's sake – if a brother wants to come back in your life and your children's lives. He should be allowed to make up for his past mistakes. There are great examples of success in this area as well.

Take the Nation of Islam, and the incredible reprogramming they've done to turn some of their members' lives around. The most notable example is El-Hajj Malik Shabazz, better known as Malcolm X. This can be done and is being done every day. The Church plays a major role in this area as well, for historically, the Church has done well in showing members love, discipline, and support, and also by showing members that they have a higher, eternal value that goes beyond what they believe about themselves. The Church can show a wealth of examples that destructive behavior does not lead to a successful life.

Of course, we are not under one religion, which is why the organization is accepting of members from all religions. While the organization acknowledges the diversity of belief systems its members will bring, it will focus on the elements of Black Unity, including financial, educational, and social elements. However, the organization will also try to have representatives of different religions available for those seeking guidance.

We should also re-institute rites-of-passage ceremonies for young men and women, so they can be taught the qualities of what it takes to be a well-rounded per-son and know what to look for when choosing a man or woman for marriage. Specific programs for young men and women can be taught to teach values and respect, in order to prepare our youth for adulthood. This would cut down on abortions, aids, herpes, STD's and divorces.

Our names should also be changed to honor where we came from and where we're going, and to continue breaking the mental chains of slavery. The first name doesn't have to be changed in honor of our parents who gave us that name, but the last name represents the slave name that we continue to pass down from generation to generation. It's time to give this up, and also give up naming our children after cars and jewelry or spelling a name differently to make it sound cooler or unique. In Africa, giving a child a name was a very special event. There were naming ceremonies where the name meant something to the family or represented something to aspire to.

We should start having naming ceremonies again in order to reconnect ourselves and our families with our African heritage, and this could be included in the rites-of-passage programs put together by the organization.

HEALTH

We must start taking better care of ourselves. According to the CDC, as a people we rank first or second in most major health categories of illnesses, including heart disease, cancer, diabetes, and obesity. That's why it's important to have our own health facilities and schools, so we can reeducate ourselves and prevent these illnesses. The organization will connect with medical clinics in the community that are already in use, and help expand on them; the organization will also foster our creation of our own health institutions. The organization will also provide assistance with us doing something we've needed to do for a long time – break bad health habits.

We have to stop smoking cigarettes. There are no benefits from them at all. Many of us started smoking them only because we wanted to act like adults. We only smoke cigarettes now because we're addicted to them. But think of the money you'll save by quitting those cigarettes, and think how you will save your health and save your family the heartache of seeing a loved one sick or dying over something that could have been prevented.

It's also time to stop eating inferior foods that our ancestors had to eat in order to survive: hog maws, chitterlings, pig's feet, and other forms of pork. These foods have very little nutritional value compared to other quality foods, and can be dangerous if not cooked properly. These foods are an example of our past negatively affecting our present and future. I know we like to turn negatives into positives and say these foods are a cultural thing now, but these foods are not healthy. How many quality meats are sold by the pound in buckets, and have to be cleaned with products including bleach, baking soda and vinegar, and then boiled, and finally covered with hot sauce to make them taste good? Many of us grew up eating pork, but that doesn't mean it was the best food for us.

If you think about our African heritage, we didn't eat a lot of meat. We should start to turn towards a more vegetarian diet, which has been proven to be a healthier diet than the way we eat now, as highlighted by the American Dietetic Association and the American Journal of Clinical Nutrition. A vegetable-centered diet would also be closer to the largely plant-based diet many in Africa still enjoy. On healthline.com you can find an article called "Diets of Africans" written in 2004 by Jens Levy and M. Christina Garces. There is great information in this article about how Africans eat today: in countries of the coast, from which many of our ancestors came, Africans eat more fish along with vegetables and some sort of grain. In countries further inland, the people eat more grains and vegetables along with small amounts of beef, goat, or chicken.

Modern vegetarian food has come a long way from just tofu and salads. There are foods now that taste just like beef, chicken and fish. There is even vegetarian cheese. Most of these products are sold in major supermarkets across the country. When you try vegetarian foods for yourself, you too will be surprised by how good they taste. You will also lose weight eating a vegetarian diet, and have less of a chance to get fat. By losing weight and eating better, you can help to prevent many of the major diseases that are plaguing our community.

Through our business pursuits, we can produce and distribute vegetarian products ourselves and save money while doing it. The organization will collaborate with companies that are already making these products, and foster our starting our own projects as well.

We need to start exercising to keep our weight down and our heart and bones strong. Obesity is a major problem in our community. Just by losing weight we could prevent, heal, or control many problems. We could become healthier even while dealing with diabetes, heart disease, arthritis, high blood pressure, and perhaps even overcome these conditions.

We can develop and utilize exercises that work the whole body in a minimum amount of time. These exercises can be developed for different sizes and age groups. We especially need to start doing this because physical education is being cut in the public schools, and our children are spending more time in front of the TV and computer. We adults also aren't as active as we once were. The organization will assist with renting out time slots for different activities like swimming at the YMCA, and the local gyms in the community, and will promote our starting our own facilities to meet our exercise needs.

Another aspect of this is forcing our children to eat everything on their plate. I believe this came from a time when we didn't know when our next meal would come, or if there was enough to eat. This isn't to say that there aren't people out there who aren't hungry; I'm talking about the tradition of overeating. This problem can be solved by not putting so much food on the plate, allowing the child to ask for more if they want more. It can also be solved by not ordering oversized options at fast food outlets as well.

Some of you may not have heard of this, but intuition is another major part of our health and general well-being that needs to be talked about and learned. Intuition is called by many names, including "gut feeling," or insight. Women are most noted for using intuition, but we all have this ability. We rarely use this gift that could save us from a lot of bad decisions and heartache.

We also need to discover and rediscover natural remedies to cure illnesses. Man-made drugs cause side effects, and rarely cure the condition they are prescribed for. Instead, these man-made drugs are designed to be taken for life. This is good for the drug companies, but not good for us, physically or financially.

We, through the organization, can partner with companies making superior, natural products that can be sold to our people and the general public. Such partnerships can be structured to bring more money into our community. We can also invest to have our own such companies. Clinics can be established in our communities, where we can get basic annual checkups. Doctors and nurses could start to do house calls again, which could overcome some of the historical reasons many Black people have for not trusting doctors and hospitals (look up the Tuskegee Experiment, for one example).

Some Black people suffer needlessly because most of us don't give blood or register to give bone marrow. We should be giving blood at least on a monthly basis. The donation process could be set up at the clinics in our community, which will allow our people to give blood more often, perhaps once a month, to meet the needs of their communities.

Drug addiction centers need to be created in our community, so we can really help our people get off drugs, instead of making another industry off of their misery. I consider alcohol a drug as well, but because alcohol is legal and is accepted in society, it is treated differently. Legal and illegal drugs have always had a devastating effect in our community. Some of our best-known personalities in politics, sports, entertainment and other areas have died because of their addiction to drugs and alcohol. We need to have places to help our people heal, recover, and grow beyond the need to depend on drugs for support and comfort.

BUSINESS AND FINANCE

When Michael Jordan, Tiger Woods, and Lebron James receive millions of dollars for endorsing particular products, we all think we are succeeding. What we don't see is that the owners of the products and the companies that make those products make billions from all of us for the few millions they give to a few Black celebrities.

This pattern needs to stop, now. When someone from outside our community wants to do business with us, we need to make sure we're getting 50 percent or more of the benefit from the venture. We must become better negotiators by knowing our value. If business people from outside the community choose not to agree with this type of arrangement, we have enough professionals to fill the void. A refusal from outside can be a new opportunity for us on the inside. We do not need to work with business people who do not want to give us our fair share of the profit we produce, when there are Black business people who can provide the same products and services and will be giving back to our community.

For example, when agents from the major sports teams are looking to sign our athletes, they should be asked, "What will you be giving back to the community?" We could also create our own shoe and clothing companies and have our athletes and entertainers own and endorse them. People will buy whatever our athletes and entertainers wear; if we had our own shoe and clothing companies, the money would come back into our communities. This would work as a form of reparations for us.

Of course we have to hold our own business people to at least the same standards to which we hold business people from outside. There are many Black businesses that are just as selfish as any outside the community, and only care about themselves. This must stop as well, if they want our business. We must make sure our own businesses are giving back to the community as much as or more than they are taking away.

Instead of reinventing the wheel, we could partner up with Black businesses that are willing to work with the organization to expand their business.

Criteria would be in place for businesses that would have to agree with giving discounts and providing the best service, along with other stipulations. Examples of areas we could partner in are food, clothing, cleaning supplies, real estate, agriculture, financial services, travel, sports, entertainment, etc. This would be a lot easier than starting from scratch, because of the expertise we would be getting from successful business owners. We would still start up new businesses with experienced people at the helm. Black experts in every field could be working to advise us, instead of new business people having to do it the old way through trial and error.

There are ways we can use our buying power to buy real estate at a discount, so more people will be able to afford a home and not worry about getting ripped off like in the sub-prime housing scandal. We could also use that same buying power to make long-term investments. This can be done through investments through which we can buy real estate from banks and new developments. This is how members and non-members will be able to invest in mortgages for long-term investments.

Networking should be a priority in our community. This is something that needs to be focused on and will be included as a part of the organization This will be developed by utilizing the Internet and functions at the organization's buildings for different groups including youths, adults, professionals, etc. Jews, Asians, Italians, and others have been networking amongst themselves since they came to the United States. We need to start doing the same, on a national and global level.

Think about the factories and services we could have across the country and the jobs they'd produce, for every product or service you use. All this and more can be done by making a conscious commitment to coming together and supporting the organization This will also be done by investing in new and existing businesses. This can easily happen by simply redirecting the way you spend your money. You're already spending this money. The question is: Are you spending it with people who are using it to help you and your people grow to be the best they can be, or are you spending it with people who are using it to help their people grow and be the best they can be?

Green technology is another way to generate new business opportunities and jobs in our community. This is a whole new area that should be capitalized on. Information on jobs and training in green technology all over the country can be posted on the organization's site. Research teams could be created across the country to connect, advise and invest in people who have ideas in this area and others. Help would also be given to patent our inventors' ideas, and market the resulting products to the public. The organization would both utilize its own facilities for these purposes, and invest in and collaborate with colleges as well.

Doing business with our brothers and sisters in Africa should be a priority for us. There is an unlimited amount of opportunity to help our brothers and sisters in Africa, and also help our communities here. We can fill the technological voids in Africa while at the same time creating opportunities for our community. There are also opportunities in the Caribbean, in countries including Haiti and Jamaica. Our people there could supplement our production of goods and services. The organization will work to set up agreements with the different countries and finding out what each needs and can do.

We should also take back some of the industries we gave up or let go. Black women should not need to go to Asians to have their nails done, for one example.

Some of you may already know that a lot of companies that exist today profited from the slave trade; consider Aetna, Fleet Boston Financial Corporation, and CSX Corporation for a start! Yet we still support these companies, partly because we don't know of all the companies that profited from our ancestors' misery, and also because we honestly haven't given the issue a lot of thought.

Some of us have a very short-term memory when it comes to dealing with serious issues in our community. I believe these are the companies we're trying to get reparations from, along with the government. As I've said before, we can get our reparations by not supporting these companies and by starting and supporting our own companies and marketing the products and services to other groups. We will never get what we deserve in the form of reparations, because if we did, we would own this country. That's not going to happen. Our only alternative is to take what we deserve by creating opportunities like affirmative action plans for ourselves.

Businesses can also be started to take advantage of certain financial markets that have a reputation for overcharging and bad service to the general public. Examples of these types of companies include banks, and insurance companies. We can take advantage of this while at the same time generating money from outside our community.

Throughout our history in this country, we have rarely focused on creating a stable economic and financial base in our community. When we were segregated, we had this stable base, but it was only because we were segregated and had no other choice, or because we were fed up with the way we were treated and decided to do something about it. It was not because it was the right thing to do for our people, in order to create a financial power base to strengthen our community. It's time to change this type of thinking and start reaping the benefits of supporting our community financially.

For example, consider the benefits that could occur from having strong Black credit unions instead of relying on the major banks. Banks are specifically set up to make the most money for their shareholders or owners, while credit unions are for members only and are set up to help their members. So, credit unions often offer higher interest rates on savings and lower rates on loans than banks do.

Just imagine the billions of dollars that can be redistributed in our favor through the use of Black credit unions! Think about our people having our own credit card, the real Black card, with a flat low interest rate, balance transfers, and no tricks used to keep you in debt forever, along with advice offered on how to get out of debt in the shortest period of time.

These are the kinds of services we could have in place. Why don't we? The money, expertise, and demand already exist. All we have to do is redirect the way we spend our money and everybody wins. The organization would win by creating jobs and securing financing for different businesses. This will keep more money in the community, and allow new businesses to be started because of the availability of loans; our money would be recycled back into our community and create more opportunities. You would personally win by getting higher interest rates on your savings account and by saving money on interest payments, which you could use to pay down your debt, and later save for a down payment to buy a home if you wanted to buy one.

How many billions do you think we can generate from this one venture? Can you imagine what we can do with that money? Credit unions could be set up by the organization in cities across the country with online access for members. The organization will also work with existing credit unions. We can add mortgages, retirement plans, car and business loans. We could also add insurance for car, home, life and health.

We can also add school loans, until we're able to provide free education to all our students. A stipulation can be added that the student would have to go to a Black college. This will allow us to keep more money in our community, and should help to eliminate the financial problems at those colleges.

We can literally create our own national health plan. Remember, Black people: we are a nation. We're just not united, yet. Each one of these services mentioned is a multi-billion dollar market. Think about all those billions of dollars going to your community and the jobs that would be created from you not spending anymore than you normally do, but by simply redirecting where you spend your money. This is not rocket science or a pipe dream. It has been done before and can be done again. The organization will foster the creation of new companies and partner with companies already doing this kind of work.

There's a book called *Black Wallstreet* by Jay Jay Wilson and Ron Wallace. In this book is the true story about a Black town in Oklahoma that was so self-sufficient, they were the envy of the white community. We have the ability to create a national Black Wall Street. Imagine an investment department that offers investment opportunities for members who want to take advantage of the new products and services offered. This is how many other groups raise money to invest. Because of the volume of investors, any losses in the ventures would be minimal.

Imagine one million members investing five hundred to a thousand dollars or more a year, in a number of different projects. That's a minimum of $500 million to work with every year, with only one million members. Now multiply that number by ten, twenty, thirty million members. Even with one million members, we could create enough opportunities to keep us all busy for a long time while all that money recycles back into our community. For example, real estate ventures can be set up to help members buy homes. With low property values and low interest rates, now is a great time to buy a home.

For another example, we could have any movie, play, video game, or other entertainment-related invention fully funded, along with all the relevant research, without a problem. We would never have to worry about not having enough money to fund anything if investors outside of our community don't get what we're trying to do. Remember: We don't need Hollywood's money to do what we need to do creatively. Hollywood needs our money. And it can be cut out of the picture. Remember the movie Spike Lee made about Malcolm X? He wasn't able to get all the money he needed from Hollywood to finish the movie, so he called some of our wealthy brothers and sisters and raised the money to complete the film. This is a perfect example of what we can do when we come together.

You don't have to be wealthy to have tremendous financial power; you just need to work with your brothers and sisters. Just by simply redirecting where we spend and invest our money, we can determine that our communities will prosper and thrive.

POLITICS AND POWER

Most Black people have been registered Democrats for decades. Yes, we have made some progress with the Democratic Party, but the masses of our people have not benefited. We are being taken advantage of in this one major area – and what sense does it make to keep voting for the same people who are taking advantage of us every year? There's a saying that if you keep doing what you're doing, you'll keep getting what you're getting.

We have to start voting strategically rather than just following party lines. Right now, the elite of our people are reaping most of the few benefits the political system offers us – but we need to insure that those we support with our votes will work to better our lives at all economic levels. One way to change this would be to become a voting block, which would allow us to play the parties against each other to get our political demands satisfied. We would be the "swing voters" who determine what candidates get into office in both parties; this would make both Democrats and Republicans have to cater to us.

I'm not talking about changing party affiliation; I'm talking about thinking independently and voting not by party lines but for the person who will address our issues, rather than who the parties want us to vote for. We need to support those who address our issues on a city, state, and federal level.

We also have to get more involved in the political system, not less, by educating ourselves and our youth in how the system works and how to use it to our advantage. Our next step would be to groom and select our own candidates. Right now, we often have to choose candidates based on name recognition, who they know, and how much money they can raise. But even within the Democratic Party we could be grooming the people we want to represent us within the party.

A political department will be created within the organization in each city and state, to educate us, groom candidates of our choosing, and encourage us to vote to get what we need. This would give us an edge on both parties.

Someone said, a sign of insanity is doing the same thing but expecting a different result. The Democrats have been getting a free ride at our expense for a while now. It's time to start making them pay. As a voting block we have the power to determine who the next president, congressman and mayor, in most major cities where we're the majority or a large group.

A lot of us were able to take advantage of the crumbs of affirmative action; now that it is being dismantled, even the crumbs are gone. White women benefited as much if not more from affirmative action than we did. But now that affirmative action is basically gone, we need to make some affirmative actions of our own by combining our political and financial power to give ourselves the oppor-tunities we need to succeed.

Imagine the power we would possess if there were an organization of twenty to forty million Black people who are united to help each other be the best we can be, physically, mentally, spiritually, and financially. Imagine the power we would possess if no political party could take us for granted, and if we had the organized buying power to get what we needed without having to go to the political system to get it. Imagine the power we would possess as an organization that can speak with one voice on the most important issues facing the Black community, an organization that, when our people are messed with, could literally shut down, close, disrupt companies, stores, and anyone else who didn't treat us with respect and fairness. This is the kind of organization we can build. This is how we will get respect, fairness and equality.

In this country and around the world, money is power, and also the only thing some people understand when it comes to showing respect and fairness. With the numbers in our organization and the hundreds of billions of dollars of disposable income we spend every year, we would have that kind of power. If you notice in the past, the only time we received respect and fairness was when we were united for a specific cause after getting fed up with the way we were treated. I gave the example earlier about the Montgomery bus boycott, and how the bus company had no choice but to let us sit wherever we wanted. The bus company had no choice because we left it no other option for staying in business.

Here's another example: remember the Texaco incident, when a meeting was recorded with executives saying inflammatory words about Black people? The media and Black organizations were notified. Texaco lost millions of dollars just on their stock alone, not including their reputation. How about Denny's, when someone in our community didn't get served? Denny's ended up spending millions to hire and retrain employees, and

Denny's had to change their policies because of what we did.

The major media organizations played a major role in these examples, and we need to start using these organizations more strategically so we can get what we need from them. Although the use of media can be a double-edged sword, we must use it and not let it use us. The Jewish people have been very good, since the Holocaust, of using the media to get what they need known across – if they can do it, so can and so should we. We also need to strengthen and support our own media organizations, and support them with our advertising dollars.

We cannot and should not wait until something major happens in our community and we get so upset that we have to unite in order to correct a problem. We should already be organized so no one would dare try and take advantage of our community. In order to have this kind of power, we need to be united and speak in one voice when it comes to major issues that affect our people. This is how you get respect.

An organization of millions can do much to change the attitudes of other groups who often take advantage of us because they know we're not united and don't speak in one voice until something major happens. We can and should change this. It's time for power – power will get you peace.

THE FUTURE

Predicting the future is not an exact science, but based on similar events and patterns in the past, you can get a good idea of how things will turn out. That's why it is so important to know your past, so that you don't repeat the negative experiences in the future. There's an old saying I've changed a little bit: if you don't know your past, you'll continue to repeat the things you don't want to happen in the future. Now is the time to act on solutions that are available to us.

Our world is changing and getting smaller every-day, and in these tough economic times, groups tend to stay together and help other group members before they help anyone else. We cannot nor should we expect other groups to help us in difficult times such as these. We know this based on previous recessions. I actually believe we are in a depression – maybe not as bad as the Great Depression, but certainly the worst economic downturn since then. There are no quick remedies, or quick fixes. It took at least eight years for the country to get into this mess and it will probably take years for the country to get out of it.

It will be up to us to help one another, as it should be. We already know that we won't be a priority when it comes to getting help from large political and business forces. That's been proven in the past by the billions in bailout money given to the banks, financial institutions and insurance companies who got us in this mess in the first place, and also by the things government is responsible for by allowing financial institutions and big business in general a free rein.

Millions of people across the country have lost jobs and are losing jobs and homes at record numbers; our people have suffered more than any other group in this crisis. Some people who have found work can only get part-time jobs, or jobs that pay half of what they were getting at their old job. We will not be the first hired back, because it's not our people that own the majority of the companies that will be hiring. Nor will we be the first to get loans to help us save our homes and businesses, because we own very few banks. The Asians won't be hiring us to work in their businesses, the Arabs won't be hiring us to work in theirs, and neither will whites, at least not until they've taken care of their own first. So where does that leave us?

Sometimes it takes a bad situation to change the way we do things, to learn from our past and set a new course for our future. There is no better time to come together physically, mentally, spiritually, and economically than now. I believe this is our time to come together and at long last create the opportunities we have created for others for ourselves.

I also believe that if we don't take advantage of this period to come together, we as a people will be in worse shape than we were in the last depression. This is not meant to scare you, but to make you realize how bleak and serious this situation is. All across the country, our people are suffering because for so many years, we've depended on other people to help us do what we should have been doing for ourselves. In the past, when things were plentiful, we were still last in receiving what we needed, but we did receive some help. Now that the economy has changed for the worse, we will probably not receive any help, or very little.

It's time for us to build an economic base on which our people can stand. By pooling our money together as a group, we will be able to come through this crisis with the least amount of pain. The sooner we start, the sooner we can help each other. Don't you think other groups are doing this, and will continue to, until they see the economy start to change? We should too. Working together can create a bright future for us with endless possibilities. Not working together will put us in a position we may never be able to recover from. We're still spending our money with every other group but our own; if we don't stop this, it will get worse in our community, and we will have no one to blame but ourselves.

Let's learn from the past, and set a new, exciting, and worthwhile course to a bright future. To get this started, you only need to follow a few steps.

1. Before we set up the organization, we need to raise money. By searching and shopping on http://www.3ufirst.com for the things you normally buy, we can begin to bring billions back to our community, and begin to solve our own problems.

2. Tell everyone you know about the book, about http://3ufirst.com, and what we're trying to do. That's it.

Now after reading about the plan which can change our lives forever, go to the conclusion part to complete the book. If after reading it, you don't feel you have enough information to do the three simple things above and need more convincing, or are interested in knowing how we became divided in the first place, then the second part of the book will give you what I think is the reason why it's so hard for us to unite and come together.

THE PROBLEM

After reading all that you have read, and if you still don't want to follow the simple steps I've laid out that will unite us and create financial freedom and happiness for yourself and our community, this is the part of the book that will address why. As I said in the introduction, I apologize if I use terms in this section of the book that may offend you. This is not my intention. It is only to stress to you the importance and seriousness of realizing why we are not united and are not reaping the benefits other groups do in order be happy and prosperous. So what is our real problem? I'd like to focus on the mental issues that have kept us from reaching our full potential and true greatness, from being the best at whatever we do as a people, collectively, not just individually.

The first thing you need to understand: your ancestors who were brought from Africa were the strongest of their people. When whites took us from the motherland, they didn't take the old or the sick; they took our warriors, farmers, and leaders. The white man knew that these strong, intelligent people could easily throw off their chains unless drastic measures were applied. So, the white man decided to use one of the oldest rules of warfare: divide and conquer. Even on the slave ships, where our ancestors were packed like sardines, care was taken to make sure that Africans from different tribes were kept separate to make sure they would not learn to speak each other's languages and communicate. (And yet, we still tried to free ourselves on the ships, as the movie *Amistad* reveals.)

When our ancestors arrived here, slave masters developed a system to keep us divided, a system that is sometimes credited to the writings of Willie Lynch. The system was designed to make us distrust one another, to set the field slave against the house slave, the dark-skinned slaves against the light-skinned slaves created by the rape of masters upon slave women. We were also punished for working together except for the benefit of the slave master, and rewarded for betraying one another to the master. These were a strategy the slave masters used to cause division amongst us, so there would be less of a chance our ancestors would try to escape or rise up together to fight the injustices and to free ourselves (although many of our ancestors still rose up, worked together, and fought for their freedom anyhow. Remember Harriet Tubman?)

When our ancestors became free as a whole, many didn't know what to do with the freedom they had, except for trying to satisfy an unquenchable thirst for the education and knowledge they were deprived of for so long because of the devastating effects of slavery. But today in many urban cities, we have a fifty percent dropout rate, or more. What happened to that thirst for education and knowledge?

The former slaves had no money, land, education, or power because the United States government didn't really want to free them in the first place. There were very few services to help the former slaves get on their feet. There were no forty acres and a mule waiting for them. No welfare or social security to help. They did have an agency called the Freedmen's Bureau, which did some positive things like help provide food, shelter, work contracts, and acted as a moderator in conflicts between Blacks and whites. The agency is noted for helping to establish Black schools in the south. But this took place over a very short period of time – only about ten years, during which time former Confederates and white agents who were supposed to help the newly freed slaves fought against the agency.

A new form of slavery came on the scene after Lincoln was assassinated. Jim Crow came into effect, which kept us separate but unequal, with very little resources to work with. When racist whites took back their control of the South, they set up Black codes to control what Blacks could do. Under these conditions, many Blacks returned to work on the same plantations they had been slaves on! Yet as the strong and powerful people we are, we still persevered. Eventually, many Black people followed jobs and opportunities out of the South into the North and West.

What I want you to understand is that there was only a very short period in which Blacks received help – only about ten years – compared to more than three hundred years of slavery and Jim Crow. Today, we don't work on farms anymore; we now wear both blue and white collars. But racism lingers to this very day. So does the negative programming we received.

In order for us to really take advantage of the opportunities we have to offer this country and the world, we need to be united. After all, it was our ancestors that worked from sunup to sunset in the fields for no pay for over three hundred years, and our inventions that made this country great, yet as a people we haven't fully benefited or prospered from any of it. Why? Most whites were not and are not interested in sharing period, because they've also been negatively programmed this way. If the majority of these kinds of whites don't own or control something, they have a problem with it. They continue to analyze us, but many whites need to start analyzing themselves to understand why they're so selfish and hypocritical.

But I'm more concerned about us understanding ourselves – a lot of us are still acting out negative programming passed down from generation to generation. Want proof of this? We still talk about the differences in the way we look. A light-skinned (some say "redbone") woman is supposed to look better than a dark-skinned woman; straight hair is supposed to be better than curly hair. In addition, we have had no national, financial, health, social, political, educational, or cultural organization with at least a million members since Marcus Garvey's movement in the 1920s. Every successful organization we had was brought down with the help of someone who looked like us. We do have large members in religious organizations, but unfortunately they are divided as well, and in the past, religious organizations were also used to keep us under control.

Another big symptom of the problem is that we rely too much on other people for our happiness. What do I mean? We expect other people to give us jobs, food, clothing, shelter, health, wealth, entertainment, and anything else you can think of (when we could be creating these opportunities for ourselves, like we had to do in the past). These expectations are not entirely our fault:

they are partially due to the negative mental programming that was put on us during slavery. I refer to this negative programming as "the slave mind" – the mindset our oppressors tried to force our people into in order to keep us under control. This mindset persists to this day.

The way we treat each other is an unfortunate legacy that continues to this day, while we wonder why we don't have much as a community compared to others, who have been in this country for a short time and have a much smaller population than us (for example, consider the resources controlled by the Black church, and how division in the Black church has hindered it from using those resources for the betterment of all our people). Look in the mirror, Black people. I'll say it again: we can no longer blame the white man for our problems now. He created them and continues to capitalize on our problems to this day, but we have continued to pass on the legacy of the slave mind, from generation to generation.

This is the main reason why we as a people don't work together as a community like other groups. Until we do, we will continue to complain to each other and ask why we are still struggling as a group. Please don't misunderstand me; I'm also included in this negative program. I'm just aware of it and trying to do something about it. But most of us are not even aware. Can we live with being programmed to never uniting, coming together to maximize our full potential? Yes, we can – we have been doing it for a long, long time. But can we as a people truly be successful with this type of negative programming, financially supporting every other group except our own?

This is one of the reasons why we're one of the largest consumer groups. We buy what we buy, wear what we wear and do what we do because it's all working on a subconscious level. The chains of slavery are not physical anymore; they're mental and a lot harder to fight because you can't see them, or don't think they exist. But you can see the results of it: a community divided by the haves and the have-nots, light skin, dark skin, straight hair, curly hair, and all the other things we allow to divide us.

Have you heard of the Willie Lynch letter? Some say it's an urban legend, but I bet some aspects of the letter are true. The methods the slave masters used to control us definitely used some of the divide and control tactics Mr. Lynch supposedly drew up for his associates. With over three hundred years to perfect the tactics, slave masters and their successors by different names definitely became experts at ways of controlling us and keeping us divided. These tactics are still being used today, just in a bigger market to include everyone, with marketing psychologists showing companies how to get us to buy and do things we really don't need or want to do (based on fostering dissatisfaction with our skin, our hair, our noses, and whatever else marks out our African heritage).

To let you know how long-lasting the effects of our programming have been, consider the results of a test done in the 1940s. Two black psychiatrists tested black children in schools in the North and South to see what they thought about themselves during the segregation period and to show how separate but equal education affected the children in the South. They were to choose between a black doll and a white doll. The psychiatrist asked different questions regarding good, bad, pretty, ugly and others to see which doll the child would choose. For everything associated with good, pretty, or positive, the majority of the children chose the white doll. For everything associated with bad, ugly, or negative, the majority of the children chose the black doll. Unfortunately there was a similar result in the northern schools as well.

An updated study was done in 2005 by Keri Davis, an independent film producer, and the same results came out. In 2010, CNN did a similar test, and the results were the same. Based on this information, I believe this problem goes deeper than being segregated because we've been so-called integrated since the Brown vs. Board of Education ruling in 1954. The bigger problem is we haven't dealt with the psychological effects of slavery, under which we were negatively programmed.

Another example of the devastating negative programming we received can be seen in what we have been taught about Jesus Christ, one of the most important figures in all of history. I think we should know that Jesus was not white or European; if you have a Bible, check the family line of Japheth (from whom Europeans descend) in Genesis 10, and then the family lines of Jesus Christ in Matthew and Luke. There is not a single person of Japheth's line in the family line of Jesus Christ. The line of Jesus Christ comes in the same family line of Abraham, Isaac, and Jacob, making him a Jew.

Furthermore, if you know anything about the history of the Middle East, there were no Europeans in that area at the time Jesus lived except for the Romans, who definitely weren't Jewish. And even today we can see that people who are native to the Middle East are not white in appearance – many are tan or brown-skinned.

The bottom line is, Jesus Christ looked more like Black people than he did like white people. Yet Black churches have statues of a white Jesus! From a psychological point of view, thinking that Jesus is white would give a white person a mental advantage of thinking they were closer to God than anyone else. It also would give people who are not white the idea that they are farther from God. This is probably why Jesus was portrayed by modern Europeans – who went out and conquered a non-white world – as white. Remember, this is all on a subconscious level. This is why it's so hard to understand and change our negative behavior towards one another. In order to change something, you have to at least know it exists.

We must make this subject a priority in order to overcome what's keeping us from controlling our minds. Control of our own thinking will enable us to control our futures. If you're happy with this type of situation (which some of you are because you've become success-ful despite of it, or you may be among those in our com-munity who have capitalized off our programming), you may not want to hear this message or be a part of the change. But if you're not comfortable with where we are now as a people or wonder why you're not as successful as you know you can be or in spite of your own personal success, then you know we need to do something about this now.

If you're still interested in reading this part of the book, then you have an idea that something's not right with Black people's thinking when it comes to Black Unity. Every excuse in the world is used not to unite. The examples are endless – "We need to integrate; whites have the power and all the jobs, so we can't piss them off, we would be doing what they did to us," and on and on. Well, integration hasn't worked all that well: because of the color of our skin, we're still segregated in many areas and are becoming more isolated every day. The wealth of this country was created by Black people, but others are still giving us hell with high unemployment and bad education. Bad education leads to high incarceration rates, and high incarceration rates lead to big business for those paid to keep us in jail.

Speaking of jail, do you ever wonder how we get all these guns and drugs in our community? We don't produce the drugs, manufacture guns, nor sell them in retail stores. Yet guns and drugs flood our communities. There's no real war on drugs. The war is on us. But what white people fail to realize is nothing in demand stays in one area. Drugs are big problems in many communities now, but if the government had really tried to stop the flow of drugs in our community, the problem may not have spread as much as it has now.

Unfortunately, crime pays. It pays judges, lawyers, police, prison guards and other industries connected to it. It is big business now to house our people and the poor in prison. When the brothers and sisters get out, they're supposed to get a second chance to start over, but no one will hire them. We as a community don't have enough businesses that would be able to give them a second chance, so they go back to doing what they did to go to jail in the first place, and the cycle continues. The system is set-up to be a revolving door for our people to go in and out of jail. We have more people in jail than China does, even though China has more than three times the population of the United States.

No matter how you slice it, we're not doing what we're supposed to be doing as a people when it comes to supporting, creating, and maintaining what we need in order to have a vibrant and productive community. What about the millions of successful Black people who benefited in all areas of life, who don't appreciate or even know about the life and death struggles our ancestors went through so we could have a chance to be successful? Our ancestors were the people who were the first in whatever field of work they strived for and had to suffer the pain of in-your-face racism – being called names, beaten up, even killed for trying to better their lives and make sure we, their children and grandchildren, wouldn't have to go through what they went through. Some of them are still alive today, but struggle physically, emotionally, and financially because they've been forgotten. What have we given back or done for them?

Maybe we don't care, or don't remember what our foreparents did for us when things weren't as they are today – or maybe both. Our foreparents were trailblazers in sports, entertainment, business, unions, and the many other different jobs you can think of that we take for granted now. Our people have excelled in every area we've been given the opportunity to participate in, considering it was not long ago we were forced to give up our seat to sit in the back of the bus, go in back doors of restaurants and hotels, able to only use colored only hotels and bathrooms. During the mid-sixties, the time of the civil rights era, when we continued to fight and finally received some sense of equality in being able to shop, eat, and sit wherever we wanted. And, we were able to get jobs outside our community. But the job opportunities in the private sector didn't really kick in until the seventies.

Unfortunately, during this period, the country was in a recession, so the only jobs we could get were government jobs. That's why today, so many of us work or want to work for the government. We knew based on the new laws, there would have been a much better chance to get a job in the government sector anyway. I bring this up because this country officially is less than three hundred years old, and out of that time, we've only had crumbs of opportunities since the seventies. That's less than fifty years, brothers and sisters. So, yes, we have come a long way, and it says something about our strength and perseverance. But collectively, we have not come as far as we would like to think. A lot of our people did become successful, but only as individuals or small sections within our community. As a people we still have issues with working together, trusting one another, and supporting each other.

Here's more proof; another example of the slave mentality is when the chance to get some opportunities to change our lives occurred, we didn't and still don't take full advantage of them. During the seventies, we took those jobs our ancestors fought and died for and moved away from our communities to live next door to people who didn't look like us and didn't want us there. When two or more Black families moved in, whites moved out. That actually wasn't so bad at first because that's how a lot of our communities were created away from the South. We did move to better living conditions, but not always at first because of where the jobs were, and because many of our people could not yet to afford to live in a better area.

Ask yourself this question: how much of your disposable income do you spend in the Black community – for example, supporting worthy causes like the United Negro College Fund, NAACP, Urban League, Black businesses in general, and other organizations? Some of you will be proud to say you do support Black businesses and these organizations and that's a good thing. Now ask yourself how much do you spend in the Black community compared to what you spend in the white community and others? Is it equal, less, or more? That is the question you should ask yourself. You could say there aren't enough Black businesses and organizations to support. But do you support the ones we do have? Many of us don't even support the Black colleges we went to, which is a crying shame. Why?

Yes, there are pockets of thriving Black communities here and there, especially in the South, but we as a people keep less than five cents out of every dollar in our community. We don't even recycle our money once in our community, while the dollar is recycled many times in other groups' communities. Every year you hear about our buying power going up and reaching close to a trillion dollars. That's right brothers and sisters; you're spending close to a trillion dollars a year. This is money we have to spend after taxes are paid. Yet we have very few, if any national banks, insurance companies, stores, health clinics, etc. And the ones we do have, we don't support as we should.

We don't have one Fortune 500 company, yet our buying power has helped to create and sustain many such companies. We're still keeping every other group rich, yet we wonder why we don't have anything. There used to be a time when we did support our own. But now, where is that money we're spending going, and who is it supporting? This is the ultimate example of the slave mind – we don't even realize we are still passing on the wealth we create to others, because we've been programmed to do this for centuries, and it's on the subconscious level. We think every other group is worth more than we are – at least that's how we spend our money. This is certainly not in our best interest, and yet it continues!

As you already know, different groups make fortunes doing business in our neighborhoods. The Chinese have a lock on the dry cleaners and many restaurants, the Arabs have many of the corner stores which we used to have, and whites have everything else. We used to own the dry cleaning business in our community. Some of you may not remember "The Jeffersons" show – that show about a Black family that lived well because they owned a dry-cleaning business was based on reality. But when we give our business and hard-earned money to other groups, some of them act like they're doing you a favor by accepting your money. They're often unfriendly, and can be downright disrespectful. That's one of the reasons why we don't get along with some of these other groups of people. Yet we still shop in their stores. Why? Think about it – we don't own any stores in our neighborhoods anymore!

Most other communities have their own banks, insurance companies, clinics, stores, etc. in their community. They own the property in their neighborhoods. That's how they're able to keep their community strong, vibrant and together, while we continue a plan of moving away from each other, or sit by while we are *forcibly* moved away from each other. Have you noticed that there is always "redevelopment" going on in our neighborhoods? You do know what urban redevelopment means right? It means kicking us Black folks out and moving someone else into our neighborhoods. This is also called gentrification. But by any name, a neighborhood that goes through the process suddenly becomes unaffordable for us. This process is happening all over the country, but it is nothing new. It's been happening for decades – but when you own the property in your neighborhood, it becomes a community, and it's a lot harder to kick you out.

That's why communities of Asians, Mexicans, Russians, Jews, etc. have not been touched as much by gentrification. They control their community, have political power, and recycle their money in their community so they can do more with less. Why don't we do this? We used to (when we really didn't have a choice because we were segregated). That's when we had strong and vibrant communities. We need to go back to that mindset, in order to capitalize like other groups have. Of course our community was poor in some parts, because we didn't have the opportunities we do now. But we were united. We had banks, insurance companies, stores, and lived next door to doctors and lawyers. We also had political power. What happened? Since we've been given the opportunity to make more money and live wherever we wanted to live, we often chose to live as far away from our people as we could and spend our money with everybody but our own. If this type of outcome doesn't reflect the thinking of mental slavery, I don't know what does.

It seems like the more time goes on, the more fragmented we get. We are the only group of people that behaves this way to this degree. It's like we're still trying to be accepted. Why? Because we're the only people who were slaves in this country. Most people came here by choice with their language and culture intact, and have different perspectives than we do. They also have their own inferiority issues to deal with as well. They may have not been slaves, but many of their countries were colonized and they were programmed to think a certain way too – but let me get back to us. We continue to focus on the wrong issues. We will never be fully integrated because people normally care for and stick with their own group, and are not eager to let people from other groups share in the benefits of their labor. We are perhaps the only exception.

Why do we continue to treat each other in ways that show we don't value one another? One of the aspects of the slave mind is that we have been taught not to love and value one another. One of the worst examples of the slave mind and self-hatred is the use of the N-word, as it's called today. I choose to say the full word, *nigger*, in order to get the full effect. I want you to understand why it's so negative to people who know its history and true meaning. This was a word that was used by the white man to denigrate us, to make us feel less than human. It was used to separate us from all other groups.

When the word *nigger* is used by our people on our people, it is disrespecting our ancestors who fought and gave their lives so that you would be respected and have a better life. There is a reason why none of our great leaders chose to use this word. They talked against using it or used it only to describe a certain type of person who was hindering the progress of the race at large. Even the great comedian Richard Pryor stopped using the word *nigger* because he finally realized how negative and destructive it was.

Yet some of us continue to this day to use the word like it's a badge of honor. But if a white man called you a nigger, you'd be ready to fight him. The fact that people from all groups follow whatever we do, including white people, and use *nigger* to describe themselves is incredible. This is but one example of the amazing power and influence we have on people – we just don't know how to use it constructively.

The word *nigger* was created in the worst period of our history, and is still used in poor and rich neighborhoods of all groups. Unfortunately it has become cool to use the word as if it were a sign of respect for some of our people. But how can a word that was used by someone else to describe us in the most horribly negative way be used centuries later as a sign of respect and love – "My *nigger*," as they say. Imagine the Jews today using a word the Germans used to describe them during the Hitler period as a sign of respect and love. It would never happen – so why would we continue to let it happen in our community? Why do we use the worst words when it comes to describing ourselves, like dog, bitch, and *nigger*? Why don't we use the best qualities to describe ourselves, like king, queen, prince, princess, brother, sister, cousin, and family?

Could this yet be another example of the leftovers from the slave mind, when we were programmed to look at each other as animals and not as human beings? Even whites were programmed to look at us as less than human. This was done to separate us from them, and a way to justify treating us worse than animals. White people considered us chattel, which really is no different then calling us cattle, except we didn't walk on four legs (but they did think we had tails hidden somewhere). Yet we continue to use these same words that were used to describe us four hundred years ago. All I can say is: Wow, that's deep.

The question to ask is: why would white people want to be like us, if they feel we're inferior to them and have nothing to offer? Why would they want to look like us, talk like us, dance like us, sing like us, shake hands like us, and anything else you can think of they copy to be like us? Why to this day they spend years still trying to figure out how our ancestors built the great pyramids and monuments in Kemet (Egypt)? Could it be we're not the inferior, lazy people they think we are? Our ancestors' slave labor made whites, and this country, among the wealthiest on the planet. Remember that movie, *A Day without a Mexican*? That was a take on how devastating the impact California would have suffered if it lost its Mexican population. But that would have been a small thing compared to what would have happened to the United States if it had not had our ancestors' slave labor and inventions – without us, this would not be the U.S.A. it is today. Without us, the United States would not be the most powerful nation on the planet, and that is a fact.

Today when you talk about the injustices from slavery and reparations, whites are quick to want us to move on and say things like that was then, this is now. They had nothing to do with it, but what they don't understand, fail to realize, or realize but don't want to admit is, all the benefits and luxuries they've received from slavery until now, are off of our ancestors' blood sweat and tears.

This is why knowledge is powerful in knowing your history, so you know the truth about who you really are and the contributions and accomplishments our people have made. This is not only here in the U.S. but in Africa and all over the world as well. To educate our children without teaching them about their great history is incomplete, unbalanced and a travesty.

There are different forms of the slave mind. The worst in my opinion is the "wanna be white" mindset. This mentality goes all the way back to the field slave who did all the dirty, back-breaking work while the house slave lived in the house with the slave master and picked up his ways, manners, and prejudices because unfortunately, this was the environment and type of programming they had to live under. This kind of division has also been passed down from generation to generation.

You know the kind of Black folks I'm talking about. It could be you and you don't even realize it.

One possible extreme example of this self-hatred was Michael Jackson. He may have had a problem with a skin color disorder, but that had nothing to do with him changing his nose, hair and jaw. But I don't blame him because he may have been an example of what can happen when you don't know your history and the beauty of your Blackness. Mr. Jackson grew up in the white fantasy world of entertainment, and in my opinion didn't really have a normal childhood. He may have fallen victim to how some white people want to make us feel that the way we look is somehow ugly.

Some of our most beautiful Black men and women have been hurt and discriminated against by their own people because of their Blackness. When a white person looks at your darkness as ugly, you would expect this because of past and present institutionalized stereotypes, but when it comes from your own people, including family members, it's a very painful experience. This is so sad, because there are white people getting sunburns and cancer just to look like us – some whites even go as far as to thicken their lips and butts to look like us. So it's a shame we don't have a clue how beautiful and powerful we really are. This is an example of the slave mind because it originated from when Black woman were raped by the slave masters and the children came out lighter and were treated better than the other slaves.

Malcolm X often explained in his speeches what happened next: sometimes a light-skinned slave forgot he was still a slave. Some light-skinned slaves thought they were better than the rest of the slaves, until they did something wrong or got too uppity. That's when the slave master would put them back in their place. Such slaves could even be sold by the wife because of jealousy. But until that happened, light-skinned slaves were allowed to act as though their white blood made them better than their darker fellow slaves. This was the beginning of the color system within our community that still exists today.

Moving forward to the present, whites feel more comfortable around light-skinned Blacks and more afraid of dark-skinned Blacks, and tend to give more opportunities to light-skinned Blacks. And I've already described how we treat one another when it comes to skin color – both whites and we ourselves continue to perpetuate more than three hundred years of this form of the slave mind.

Within this set of Blacks, there are some that, like the light-skinned slaves of the past, have forgotten who they are. They think they're above the rest of us, thinking they're white and getting caught up in the same stereotypes some white people have about us. These people – some call them Uncle Toms – want to be white so bad; they'll do anything to separate themselves from Black people. They have totally given up on being Black and look at it as a curse. They want to disassociate themselves from us even to the point of going as far as becoming spokespersons for white people, telling them what is wrong with our communities without offering any concrete solutions. These Blacks refuse to see any racism or discrimination – basically they see what they want to see, in order to prove they are not like us. They even change the way they look, to a more extreme form than many of us do – bleaching their face, changing their nose, and even going as far as to make sure if they are dark-skinned, not to allow their children to associate with or marry another dark-skinned person. They even have clubs and organizations that cater to this type of mentality.

But where does this mentality come from, and how does it persist in the face of stark reality? To this day we aren't fully accepted as American citizens. Every other day on the news, you hear about one of us receiving some form of discrimination based on the color of our skin.

Remember Harvard professor Henry Gates who was arrested for complaining about going into his own house or the young brother Oscar Grant shot in the back while lying face down on the floor with four cops around him. We've all heard about the infamous Rodney King beating, famous Black men not being able to get a cab, and DWB, driving while Black.

Remember when Oprah Winfrey tried to shop at an exclusive store in Europe, but it was closed? They didn't see the top talk show host in the world; they saw a Black woman who had the nerve to ask them to open their store for her. You can be one of the wealthiest and famous Black people in the world, and still be disrespected. How do you think that made Miss Winfrey feel, as one of the most powerful people in entertainment? She did get the president of the store's parent company to come on her show and apologize, but the damage had been done.

These are only the cases and kinds of cases that make the news, but we know there are many more that don't get reported. Blacks and whites live in two different worlds when it comes to justice, respect, and equality, no matter who you are or how much money an individual may have. But those of us who are afflicted with the "wanna be white" form of the slave mind are willfully blind to all of this.

There is another form of the slave mind: the "ghetto slave" mindset. Some of these Black people stayed behind, and some moved, but wherever they were, they kept their mindset – even in the suburbs, they don't keep up their property; they disrespect their neighbors by playing their music loud, cursing, adding more crime, and basically doing what they did in the ghetto. These Blacks also date back to the time of slavery, and made life hard for the rest of our ancestors. Some of these were the ones who worked in the fields and were jealous of the slaves that worked in the house, and let their jealousy turn to bitterness and hatred for any slave who was doing better than they were. These are the ones that, during the time of Jim Crow, felt that since they couldn't own anything, they weren't going to be responsible for anything or anyone – they were just going to do what felt good to them at the time, and it was too bad if anybody who wasn't white and could stop them had a problem.

These are the Blacks who, through the centuries since slavery, have probably killed more Black people than the Ku Klux Klan did in their heyday. These Blacks are killing each other over colors, what street they live on, drugs and any other ridiculous thing you can think of to take a life. They stay in their neighborhoods to wreak havoc on their own people, but they won't dare go to white or any other groups' neighborhood to do this. They call themselves niggers, as if that were their given name. They will sell out their leaders because of jealousy. They are also ashamed of who they are, and will also change their appearance to look white. (Do you remember the Jheri curl?)

Many Blacks with this mindset grew up in a negative environment where negativity was the norm and not the exception. I'm not making any excuses, but part of this is not their fault. When you're surrounded by negativity, some is bound to rub off on you. But the cycle of this form of the slave mind can be broken because all they need sometimes is to see another, positive, Black-affirming alternative. Given the right opportunity and positive community support, they can change their ways (whereas those with the "wanna be white" form of the slave mind usually don't want to change). This is what makes organizations like the Nation of Islam so powerful because they show the Black man and woman another way to be who they really are.

Today, it is not usually the first generation of Blacks that benefited from civil rights acting out the "ghetto slave" mindset; it is the next two generations that have continued this pattern. The first generation worked hard, sacrificed, and struggled to save enough money for a down payment on a house in the suburbs, which were often in white neighborhoods, in order to finally have that so called American dream and give their children a better chance to succeed – but that generation has then had to watch many of the Blacks with more opportunities move away, and then see their own children and children's children, whose impressions are of growing up in yet another abandoned community, tear the community down. In all fairness to some Blacks who moved away, they were probably outnumbered in trying to change the mentality of their ghetto-minded neighbors.

With all their sacrificing and hard work, many of the first generation of Black people who could and did move to the suburbs forgot one thing: they didn't make time to pass down those values and traditions that helped them achieve their goals, and they did not have the support of a Black community that was going to help raise their children in the traditional values. This left the children to run wild in the streets and pick up the worst the streets had to offer. So instead of living in a nice, clean, quiet community, the first generation often ended up living in beautiful homes with the ghetto slave mentality right outside their doors. I have first-hand knowledge of this because I was one of those second-generation knuckleheads with the same ghetto slave mentality. I saw my nice, quiet neighborhood transform into "the 'hood" – the very thing my family was trying to escape.

Then there are some Blacks that have a combination of the two slave mentalities I've mentioned, and float back and forth between the two. When they are around whites, they act one way, and when they are around Blacks, they act another way. They use the word nigger in conversations when they're around their own people, but would never think of using it if they had the same conversation with their own people around white people (in contrast to the ghetto slave-minded people, who could care less who's around -- they're the ones you hear using the word on the bus and trains).

The combination of these two slave minds can lead to tragic consequences. In this group you'll find the people who did horrible experiments on us like the Tuskegee Experiment in order to get support from the white man – even if the experiment did start out as a worthy cause in trying to get help for men who had syphilis. Blacks affected with the combination of slave minds are the ones who most often weaken our organizations, and who make it hard for our leaders to succeed. A conscious Black man or woman who knows who they are doesn't act like this, but a double-minded Black man or woman is unreliable in their choices and actions. This type of mindset also has its roots in slavery, and continues today.

There are probably other blends of the slave mind, but I'm not a psychiatrist. I'm coming from a layman's point of view based on what I've read about and experienced (there are some books on this subject that are in the reference section if you want to research further). But what I'm saying should not be new to anyone. We've all seen and heard about these people. Some of us are these people. This is why it's so important for us to change the way we think, because it divides us from the people who are the examples of what we do right in the community.

This leads me to the next group – there are those of us who are free or almost free from the slave mind. These Blacks know their history and are some of the leaders of our community. These are ones who try to bring us together, or just live upstanding lives with strong values and traditions, support the community, and are good examples of who we really are. They're proud of who they are as Black people and don't mind saying so.

These are the people all of us need to be like – and there is still hope that we can achieve this level of true freedom, together. Certainly, we are in desperate need of such a mental transformation.

Because we were not aware of and had not dealt with the slave mind when the civil rights era dawned, we may have been set back, in the sense that we didn't take full advantage of the opportunities to build and strengthen our own communities so that we owned our property and had a strong political base. Other examples of the slave mind still in operation are in sports and entertainment. I'm going to spend some time on this in this section, because in sports and entertainment we find glaring examples of us giving up our best and brightest to be part of organizations that really didn't want us in the first place.

Sports and Entertainment

Let's talk about The Negro Leagues. We had our own baseball teams and some of the best players in the world, but because we were segregated at the time and not allowed to play in the so-called majors, we had to create our own ballparks for people to come and see our players. To prove how good we were, games were set up against the best in the so called major leagues and we would beat them. That's how the white owners found out how good we were. At first they didn't even take our best players. They took the ones they felt could fit in, not cause trouble, and prove that they had the same upstanding qualities as anyone else.

That's one of the reasons why Mr. Jackie Robinson was one of the first players chosen to play in the majors.

Although he was not a passive person, it took more strength for him not to do anything than to attack after the insults he would get, insults a lot of the older more talented Black players wouldn't stand for. After Mr. Robinson's success, they started bringing in other players until the Negro Leagues was nothing more than a part of our history. A lot of money was made in the Negro Leagues, but not as much as in the white leagues because we didn't have a lot of money and whites had bigger ball parks and crowds. But our League created jobs for a lot of our people and the money stayed in the Black community, which created other opportunities. The Negro League Baseball Museum located in Kansas City, Missouri, was created by former players.

But other than the museum, the only things we have left of the Negro Leagues are the souvenirs we wear on our backs and head, to remind us of the great teams and players who never made it to the so-called majors. What makes this story even worse is the fact that the same white organizations that didn't want us to be a part of their league (until they saw the potential to win more games and make more money) are the same people controlling part of the sales of the Negro League organization. The Black leagues were genius enough to trademark the logos of the Negro League teams, and they license companies to sell the clothes. But the major leagues control a large part of the distribution, and when people buy Negro Leagues merchandise from the major league distributors and outlets, the major leagues donate only a portion of the proceeds to former players of the Negro Leagues. What nerve. That's disgraceful.

To their credit, the creators of the Negro League Museum searched for former players and got the MLB to give pensions to them. So what has happened is not all bad, but I believe the museum's creators should have total control of those pension funds, because if it were not for them, we would probably never have heard of the Negro Leagues, just like we have lost so many other areas of our history.

In Black college basketball, a similar thing happened. During the 30s, 40s, and 50s, Black colleges prospered and were very successful, but were only allowed to play amongst themselves until they played in a special game against a white college. Well, you know what the results were. We kicked the white college team's butts, and then were allowed to play in the white tournaments, and for the College championship.

There was a catch, of course: Only one team from the Black colleges could play in the tournament. So this eliminated the rest of the Black colleges. I wonder why? We had to play against each other in order to see who would represent all of the Black colleges. The results were the same; we kicked the white college's butts and won the championship. This was well-documented in the ESPN film special *Black Magic*.

So what happened after the white college coaches saw how good we were? The same old story; formerly all-white colleges – institutions that would not be bothered with educating us in the past – took our best players. This left the Black colleges no longer able to compete with white colleges, which cut out successful recruiting for Black coaches.

College basketball is a billion-dollar business now, under the disguise of student athletics. All those billions are provided by the free labor of African American students. Does this sound familiar? Talk about modern-day slaves. And by the way, basketball won't let you go pro out of high school, even if you have the skills to do so. Why is that?

In baseball, you can go straight to the pros from high school. In tennis, you can go pro while you are in your early teens. It is harder to go into professional football from high school because of the physical ability you need to play the game, so a college-only requirement makes a little sense in football (but players with the ability also should be allowed to go pro from high school, in my opinion). But consider this information from "Diversity Disparities Racist, Except in Sports," an article by Walter E. Williams: Professional baseball is about 20 percent Black and football is about 65-70 percent Black, while the NBA is around 80 percent Black. How is it that only in the sport in which 8 out 10 players are Black, there is a rule that says players can't be accepted into a position to earn a living as soon as they have the skills to do so? I think this is morally wrong, and should be legally wrong as well.

Perhaps the NBA put in the rule that high school players could no longer go straight to the NBA from high school to keep the colleges from losing free labor and money. Considering that a young basketball player only has to go to college for one year, how much education would a player really get if he is totally focused on basketball?

I know some of you who are reading think the players should stay in school anyway. But if the purpose of going to school is to get a good education in order to get a good job, and you already have a skill that will pay you millions, why should you be forced to go to school? (This may be backfiring now because some players are going overseas to play, and are getting paid for it.) The players can always put money aside for college if the pros don't work out, and if the NBA really cared about the players, they would require that part of a player's salary be set aside in an education fund instead of preventing these players from making a living and helping their families and communities as soon as they are qualified to do so.

We're not talking about sending a generation out of school early, by the way – best high school players would get a chance to go pro out of high school anyway, and there are only about ten players or less in this category every year according to Wikipedia. But these few are the marquee players who bring in millions to elite colleges before these players move on to the NBA.

We also had our own Black professional basketball leagues because we weren't allowed to play in the NBA – that is, until NBA coaches saw us play against some of their teams and saw the potential to win more games and make more money. So of course you know what happened next. The NBA owners took our best players and the Black basketball leagues became history – our leagues actually became lost in history until former NBA great Kareem Abdul Jabbar did the documentary film, *On the Shoulders of Giants*, about it.

Did you know we had our own golf league? Guess what happened to that organization -- exactly the same thing that happened to all the other leagues we once had. Another part of our history lost is that we had a professional hockey league – yes, ice hockey. Remember, there are a lot of Blacks in Canada because Canada abolished slavery long before the United States did, and many former slaves escaped to Canada. Some of the many Black people in Canada played ice hockey – and they played it so well that the NHL actually copied their setup, as reported in the book *Black ICE – The Lost History of the Colored Hockey League of the Maritimes 1895-1925*, written by George Robert Fosty.

My point is, we made it to the white-owned major leagues because we were the best at what we did, and could give the owners of these organizations more wins and a lot more money. But what happened to our owners, our ball fields, and the money and jobs they created after our best athletes left what they had behind? When are we going to start realizing our value?

Today, it is hard to believe that Black athletes weren't allowed to play in major league sports because of how completely Black players have dominated so many sports. But remember that at one time, whites thought we didn't have the intelligence and skills to compete with them. You can still see some remnants of this: just in the last twenty years the NFL started allowing Blacks to play the quarterback position, and to become coaches. There still aren't a lot of Black owners in any sport.

In areas away from sports and entertainment, many whites – and other groups – still feel that we are inferior to them. This is why it is so important for us to know our history in all its aspects.

In entertainment a similar pattern emerged for Black people; whites wanted to be entertained by our best performers, and brought them to the best white clubs – but Black customers were not allowed in those same white clubs. It was all right for us to entertain whites, but not to socialize with them. But guess what happened when our best entertainers no longer came to our clubs, where anyone was allowed in? Some of our clubs went the same way that our major leagues went – into history. This process still occurs through what our entertainers choose to endorse. It occurs through other forms as well.

Now you may say our best athletes and entertainers made the moves that they did because there was more money to be made. That is true to a certain degree. But what did we give up for this money, and who benefited the most? Was it worth it? I think not. Our history in these areas speaks for itself. The most important things we had were our community and ownership in the fruits of our labor – unity and power. But we exchanged these things for more money – for that was the only thing we received.

A perfect example of us not knowing our value was an article in *Fortune* magazine in 1998 about how much money companies made off of former NBA superstar Michael Jordan. Now let's keep it real: what is the percentage of Black people who read *Fortune* magazine? Most of us did not find out that a number of companies made at least a total of ten billion dollars off of Mr. Jordan – and that was a low estimate. Nike alone made billions off Mr. Jordan, and is still making money today. You would think, based on this article, Mr. Jordan should have been the first Black billionaire. But in my opinion, he didn't know his value or what he was worth to the people he endorsed and made money for. The people who advised him may not have known (or cared) to help him realize his value to himself or his own people.

From Michael Jordan to Lebron James, the movement of a large portion of Black-generated wealth almost completely to the white establishment is still going on, and will continue until we wake up and change it. I will say this: a few of us are getting wise to the game. Lebron James has his own company now, the LRMR Marketing Company. Mr. James is doing the right thing: He did transfer a lot of wealth away from himself, but at least he realized his value in a very short period, and can now profit from it, instead of other people making the lion's share off of his hard work. Apparently, he is getting good advice from people that know their stuff and care about him.

Leaving aside the rare example of Lebron James taking his worth into his own hands, consider the situation we are now in concerning our athletes. Do you see a pattern, a very old pattern, here? Professional basketball and football along with college football and basketball are all multi-billion dollar markets, and I would go as far to say that if there were a majority of Blacks dominating college baseball, it would be a multi-billion dollar market as well. My question to us is: Who is benefiting from all these billions? Yes, the players are getting paid millions now, but who is really benefiting and taking in the lion's share? THE OWNERS. Out of all sports, how many Black owners are there? None in baseball and football, and only one in basketball. So, the white establishment built around sports and entertainment is making billions and billions and billions off our labor – and free labor in college. Does this sound familiar? Only white slave owners, perhaps, had a better setup for themselves!

Let's talk about entertainment, another multi-billion dollar market with Black entertainers at the top in almost every category. How many Black record labels, arenas, and theaters do we own? We do something no other group of people would ever think of doing on the scale that we do, which is to leave our own community to entertain another community that could not have cared less about us, until it found a new way to make money off of us. Look how successful the Magic Johnson theaters and Starbucks that were built in our neighborhoods are. Why couldn't we have put more theaters and quality coffee shops in our neighborhoods? We knew we needed them. But other than Magic Johnson, it seems that the rest of us keep choosing to spend our money with people who don't look like us. So, the bulk of the money once again leaves the Black community – and supports who?

But we never question this because of the money a few have made, and because we have been programmed to be the biggest consumers on the planet. We save very little if any money, we live paycheck to paycheck, and what we do produce, we give right back to the people who then make more money off us. This is also why you hear about successful athletes and entertainers losing their fortunes because of bad management – our most talented people may have a lot of money for a little while, but most don't have a clue what to do with it. They, like most of us, buy things that lose value rather than investing in things that create value in their community. So often, the purchasing and entertainment choices of our most talented individuals reflects the same poor judgment that the rest of us so often use – the only difference is that they have so much more to lose.

The Problem Continues

Most of us bought into this so-called American dream and a lot of us have prospered. But we have not prospered as a people. It doesn't matter whether you're rich or poor as a Black person; as a people, we are still treated as less than first-class citizens. To this day, we have followed the rules and done everything we could in order to be accepted and prosperous. Yet we continue to struggle as a people to gain the wealth and power we need to secure a prosperous future.

Politics is another example of people taking advantage of us, and although all Americans have been taken advantage of at times, my main concern is with *us* right now. A lot of our political struggle has to do with the way we understand – or misunderstand – the nature of American politics.

At the beginning of our political lives as a people, many of our foreparents became Republicans because Lincoln freed the slaves, but he only did it because the South would not return to the Union. I found this out about fifteen years ago when I watched the PBS special, *The Civil War*. It blew me away to think I admired this man because of what I thought he did for us, when in fact he would have kept us as slaves if the South had not seceded from the Union. (Don't take my word for it. Watch it for yourselves. As a matter of fact, the North probably wouldn't have won the war if it wasn't for our ancestors. The North was losing and finally decided they needed to enlist our people.) Now consider: we as a people made our first major political decision based on the lie that one president and his party cared about us as a people. That pattern of making political decisions based on misinformation continues.

Eventually, we jumped on the Democratic bandwagon, and yes, some things did change under their watch, but now, we all know that we're being used by the Democrats. We vote for them every year, with little to nothing to show for it. The Democrats know that we're not united and don't speak with one voice, so they continue to give us crumbs and we continue to accept those crumbs. We tell ourselves that we are voting for "the lesser of the two evils." Meanwhile, we like to brag and say that we're not monolithic or don't speak as one – when what we need is to speak as one, just like most other groups.

We don't have to agree on everything, just the most important things like how to build an economic base that will enable us to build a strong, self-reliant community. It's time we start relying on ourselves to provide for the things we need – we did this in the past. Why don't we do this now?

I believe the slave mind is the root of all our problems. Very few have addressed this most important issue on the level it needs to be addressed, and until we do, we will continue to suffer and struggle. We will continue as a people to be segregated within our own community and never be able to reap the full benefits of what we can achieve working together. Our inability to work together is the only thing stopping us from reaching our full potential – not just individually, but collectively.

What about equality? How can we be equal when we give what we have to people who don't look like us, and allow them to control all aspects of our lives like food, clothing, shelter, and jobs? What's wrong with this picture, Black people? Whenever someone in our community needs help, they have to go searching here and there to even have a chance to find help, because those who have the information don't want to share it. There are many of our people who will go out of their way to help, but they are the exception, not the rule.

You've heard people say things like, "I had to work hard for what I have, and so do you," or, "It took a long time for me to get this information and now you just want me to hand it to you." But I'm not talking about doing everything for a person who needs help; I'm talking about guiding the person so they can avoid some of the mistakes that were made in the past. When other groups need help, their people jump at the chance to help because they know how hard it is to make it, and want to make it as easy as possible for all of their people. They also know that by helping others in the community, they're actually helping themselves by enlarging their network and raising more money and resources for their community. We may not want to make it hard for our people, but generally speaking, we won't go out of our way to help them.

But instead, we continue to believe we are without value. Men and women are choosing each other based entirely on superficial things like looks, bling (the street name for jewelry), and how well they perform in bed. No wonder why our relationships fall apart and we can't get together on anything. Some of our women are killing – excuse me, that wasn't the politically correct word to use – aborting their babies, and using abortion like a birth control pill. Others of our women are deciding that they can raise their families just fine without a father, and choosing to leave the man out. The history of men abandoning their wives and children goes back to when we were first freed, but has become a way of life now for many men. Others of us – both men and women – have abandoned our children to grow up in the foster care system, or be adopted by people who don't look like them – whereas in the past, if the parents couldn't take care of a child, the extended family did. Some of that still goes on, but more of our children are being raised by the foster care system, or in group homes now.

We used to be able to talk to the young people, and punish them when they did wrong. Now we're afraid to because their parents might get offended, or the child may do something. What are our so-called leaders doing about this, other than talking about it? Is the problem getting better or worse? Are we headed in the right direction as a people to be respected and admired, other then in sports and entertainment? These are some major problems that we as a people need to put all our efforts in to address and change. The only communities we have are the ghettos where we live, but don't own anything and continue to be moved around because of urban redevelopment.

We are killing, robbing, and drugging ourselves at alarming rates, while outside groups are capitalizing on this by creating industries off our misery. Our values are all screwed up. Do you wonder why people treat us the way they do? They see how we talk about and treat each other! Something is not right with us.

We had better wake up, because time is running out. The middle class is being destroyed by taxes, inflation, and lower wages. Pretty soon there will only be two classes: the rich and those working for them. This economic downturn is often called the Great Recession, but don't be fooled: we're in a depression. The government will never tell you how bad it really is. The good jobs have been shipped overseas for years, so big corporations can make more profits. They even allow foreigners to come to this country to work, claiming there aren't enough qualified people here. China has become the world's manufacturer; unions are not as strong as they used to be, partly because of their own greed and corruption.

The medical field is still a strong sector, largely because of how poorly we take care of our health. Another huge industry created to keep us sick, in my opinion. Blue-collar jobs are still available, but we have to be a part of trade unions to get good jobs and benefits. A lot of these unions are still racist and will look after their own – still mostly white – before helping you. The good old boy network is alive and well.

Professional careers are still available, but you need a good education, which is getting out of reach for Black students without help or without going into serious debt. You also need a good education from the start, which a lot of our children aren't receiving. Affirmative action got us in the door, but that door closes whenever there is a recession – and we're in the greatest recession since the Great Depression, to hear the media tell it (but I just told you: we're in a depression).

So what's left – low-paying service jobs? People are losing their jobs and getting new jobs that pay half of what they used to make, if they are lucky enough to even get a job. And that's how it is in the *white* community, so how bad do you think it is in the Black community? You already know it's a whole lot worse for our people, but we are often deluded by the myth that everything is equal.

All over the world, including here in the U.S.A., people are becoming less and less tolerant of people who don't look and speak like them. There are fewer jobs and opportunities to go around. But it's time to stop playing the victim game. Yes, we are victims of prejudice and racism, but we must try a different strategy, because a lot of the victims who are competing with us are middle-class whites. So the old strategy will only get us crumbs – but the crumbs are running out. The new strategy must be about economics and finances, which is a more effective approach to getting what we need in order to accomplish our goals. This is why the solution part of this book is so important. Brothers and sisters, we hold our destiny in our own hands, and it's time to take action now.

The bottom line is, either you're helping to build and support someone else's community, or you're helping to build and support your own. It's that simple. We do have choices now.

Your programming determines what communities you're supporting. Since as a people we didn't program ourselves, and rarely control or own anything in our neighborhoods, you should already know who you're supporting when you don't think about where you are spending your money. Right now, ninety-five cents out of every dollar we spend goes to supporting mainly the Asian, Arab, Mexican, and white communities.

Let me ask you this: which one of those groups is building, supporting, and spending ninety five-cents out of every dollar in our community? The Jews recycle their money twelve times before it leaves their community, the Asians around nine times, Latinos six times, and whites unlimited (since they own almost everything), according to "Goal of recycling Black spending still a distant dream," an article appearing in 2011 in *The Louisiana Weekly*. The article also points out that we don't even recycle our money once. Why? If you don't think this is another glaring example of the slave mind, you can stop reading now and throw this book away.

There's a saying: "if you keep doing what you're doing, you'll keep getting what you're getting." I'd like to add to that saying: "You'll keep getting what you're getting, and even worse." It's time to wake up, Black people.

There are plenty of statistics, books, and other examples that prove my point about how we treat one another. I'm not trying to be right for the sake of being right. I just want to show you, we can do more united than divided.

If you have read this far and you still don't get it, or don't believe we have this problem, you've just proved my point. You still have the slave mind; you just don't know it.

Let me remind you of some of the symptoms that show we still have the slave mind. We are one of the largest consumer groups on the planet of other people's products and services, while our own schools, businesses and organizations struggle to survive. We have no Fortune 500 companies, yet we've helped to create and maintain many of them. We do not have a single national organization of any kind with at least a million members. We still focus on how dark or light-skinned we are, or whether our hair is straight or curly. We are still frying and dying our hair blonde to look like the descendants of our former masters. We are still eating the same unhealthy scraps of inferior foods our former slave masters gave us, which we now lovingly call soul food – despite the fact that this food is contributing to us having the highest rates of heart disease, diabetes, cancer, and high blood pressure. We still call each other *nigger*, a name our slave masters called our ancestors to remind us that they had total control over us and were their property. Yet we use this same word like a badge of honor either to show our affection for each other, and to show that we still believe the worst about ourselves.

Are you ready to break the mental chains? Are you going to continue to suffer needlessly, while waiting for things to get better? Are you going to continue to depend on other people for your job security and happiness, or are you going to be part of a new awakening that only requires a mental shift in where you spend your money and who you spend it with in order to create our own businesses and job opportunities? I'm talking about creating our own affirmative action programs, just like every other group does.

Our ancestors' physical and mental labor built this country to make it one of the greatest countries in the world. It's time we use the same physical and mental labor to finally create opportunities for ourselves. There will also be other books, and places to go online in the reference section, that will give you more information on these major issues.

We've been in and still are in a period of institutional racism (many white people are racist and don't even know it, because they've been conditioned to be and have built it into the way they set up the institutions of society) and negative programming under which we do things we're not conscious of. We may say one thing about loving our people, but do things that harm our people because the programming is so ingrained in us, we don't even know we're doing it. This goes for many groups of people, but my main concern is with our people. It is our time to break the chains of negative programming and become what we are destined to be as a strong, united, powerful people.

A PERSONAL MESSAGE
TO MY BROTHERS AND
SISTERS IN AFRICA

Black Africa, this book is for you too. The Motherland is a super-rich continent. Yet a lot of you African brothers and sisters are struggling to survive – so much so that you're leaving your countries to come to this country, which your ancestors built and made the most powerful country in the world. But why would you leave Africa, a land rich in every resource you can imagine?

I know that part of the reason is the colonization of Africa, when countries were divided up amongst European nations, European nations that began an era of raping and pillaging the human and natural resources of the Continent. This raping and pillaging continues to this day, in the form of corrupt and greedy governments choosing to satisfy their own individual needs rather than the needs of their people. This is an example of the colonial mind that still exists in Africa -- a mindset that shows itself here in the United States in the division that has been fostered between Africans and African Americans.

But in fact, we as Black people are the same boat. We should be taking advantage of the best we both have to offer. We should be working together, using our resources to build a better future for all of us. These same European countries that colonized Africa still have a hand in the control of all our Black people, by controlling the resources of your Continent and keeping you in debt. This couldn't be done without the help of these so-called leaders of your people – how are your leaders leading you right while you continue to suffer so the rest of the world can live off the resources of Africa. Something is wrong with this picture.

I find it hard to understand how your countries could be in debt considering all the physical and mental resources Europeans took for centuries from Africa in order to make Europe rich and prosperous. It's funny how when Africa's countries became independent from European control, the Europeans wanted to start on an equal footing, without having to give anything back. Very little has been done to fix the devastation they caused and are still causing. And then they have the nerve to loan you money to fix problems they created. That's like stealing from you and then selling you back your own property. Europeans should be paying you, not the other way around.

How did African countries with vast amounts of physical and mental resources become poor and in debt in the first place? Why are they still in debt after decades of loans, and who's benefiting the most from these deals? Europeans are at fault! How about demanding reparations from them?

(I must admit I don't know as much about African history as I do about the state of Africans here in the United States. If I'm not completely correct in my take on things, please forgive me. And please believe that I am saying what I am saying to you out of love and deep concern.)

The other part of what is holding you back is the psychological effects of colonialism, similar to the psychological effects of slavery here in America. I believe what is true for Black people here in the United States are true for you in Africa (and also when you immigrate here). You too need to understand how negative programming has affected you and still affects you today – a major symptom is the tribal and class division and strife that continues to weaken Africa's many countries.

The difference between what your ancestors went through and what mine went through is only that your ancestors weren't slaves, slaves who were treated in the most inhumane ways possible. I'm not downplaying the atrocities that your ancestors endured in Africa, and the suffering you are enduring this day at the hand of traitors among your own people. But your ancestors, and you, have an advantage: you have been able to keep your languages, cultures, and communities. Black people in America were stripped of everything, and had to cling to what was remembered and passed down by word of mouth of the spirit of our ancestors, in order to keep what was left of our culture. This means that you start from a less difficult position than we do – what will work for African Americans in coming together may work even better for you!

My African brothers and sisters, you will not reach your full potential until you break the mental shackles that still control and divide your people. You need to understand your value as well, and set up deals that benefit you more than the outsiders who are in Africa. You in the Motherland need to understand that we are all in the same boat and can follow a similar path to the solution for our people's unity, prosperity, and happiness. In a sense you have a further advantage; you can take back control of your countries, and some of you have already done this!

You need to start working together across tongues, tribes, and nations, by taking the best of what each country has to offer and implementing it in every country on the Continent. It's time to think about the unity of the nations, rather allowing yourself to be divided into and dealt with as individual tribes – and also to think of the unity of the Continent, and not merely of your individual nations. Think about who benefits from your many divisions! Is it the nation, a few communities within the nation, and a few individuals in the community? Is it people living far away, in the same region of the world that profited from putting your countries through hundreds of years of colonization and hundreds of years of stealing and selling some of the best of your Continent's people into slavery?

Here is how you can tell if your country is still under the rule of its oppressors even though the oppressors are not physically on the scene. Think about how long it's been since your country was ruled by an outside nation, then compare how you are living now compared to you or your elders were living then. Then compare how whites are living now in your countries compared to how they lived in the colonial past. I'm just pointing out the long-lasting hold of colonialism that still exists today. In a way, your condition and ours as Africans in America are similar.

There are some success stories in Africa, stories of how countries have taken back and redirected their resources to benefit all of the people, not just a few individuals

– and wealthier African countries should be lending to other African countries in need. In that way, you would keep the money recycling on the Continent rather than sending that money to countries that are only interested in taking your resources and keeping you in debt.

You also need to reconnect with your brothers and sisters in the United States. We can help each other in so many ways. You wouldn't have to worry about getting ripped off because we in the organization recognize that we have so much in common with you and truly want to help you.

From Africa to America, Black people have survived and are still surviving the atrocities of slavery and colonialism, but we must do more than survive. It's time to break away from the European mind-control that continues to hold us back. We must come together in order to fulfill our destiny as a great people again, and go back to our successful African ways while connecting with each other to help all our people everywhere to be the best they can be, so we can all reach our full potential.

FEAR

I know a lot of you want to get involved with the organization, but are afraid for many reasons. You're afraid of change, afraid of what the repercussions will be for aligning yourselves with this organization, afraid you will lose your money, and afraid of other things as well. In this brief chapter, I'd like to address your major fears.

In general, change for the most part is a good thing. The problem is we get comfortable with the way things are because we're creatures of habit. So when we have to do something different, it always seems dramatic and uncomfortable. But once we have changed, the change we have made becomes the norm and we become comfortable again. So don't worry: supporting your people through the organization will soon be a natural, welcome part of your life.

As far as repercussions are concerned, none of them could be more serious than what we as a people are going through right now. Our unemployment rate is more than double that of whites. We have higher rates of crime, illness, and disunity than any other group, rates that will continue to get worse if we don't do anything other than what we are doing now. By joining and supporting this organization, we can finally start to change these problems on a national level that will benefit us all. Our main problem now is us and the way we think. We have everything we need in our community to be a happy and prosperous people. We just need to put ourselves first for once; the benefits far outweigh any possible repercussions from outside forces.

Last but not least, some of you are afraid of losing your money. But let's be real: We waste money on things that have little to no value every day, so even if you joined the organization and lost all your membership money (which, if you make the two-year commitment, costs less than a cup of coffee a day) isn't it worth taking the chance to unite as a people, to bring back some of those billions we spend with other groups, to re-educate and educate ourselves and our children in order to help us become the best we can be, to create opportunities for our people so we don't have to depend on anyone but ourselves? Don't you think this is worth trying?

There are many examples in history and everyday life of people becoming successful when they have overcome their fears. And remember: fear is often our reaction to the thought of doing something, to the thought of breaking a comfortable habit. But it is not a reliable, rational reaction to actually doing what needs to be done. Let's not allow our fears to stop us from doing what we need to do in order to make our communities the success they deserve to be.

CONCLUSION

If you've read this far, you realize the unlimited potential this organization has to offer you, and our people. Hopefully you also realize this will not happen overnight. We're talking about building our own institutions – that will take time. But the reprogramming of the slave mind may take even more time, particularly since many of you may not believe we have this problem as a people (but the examples I've given in "The Problem" speak for themselves). Even if you don't believe the majority of us have the slave mind, you should realize that we can do a lot more together than apart and that's what is most important.

The sooner we can start this quiet revolution, the better off we will all be. Some of you may say that we wouldn't have gotten as far as we have, without trying to integrate into the different areas, but I think it would have been better if we stayed together and built up our own community first. The reason being, whites were forced to accept us through laws the majority of them didn't agree with. They didn't feel the need to practice what they preached, that all men were created equal and treat an individual based on their character rather than the color of their skin.

We really don't know what would've happened if we stayed together, but there are examples here and there that have been successes where we stayed together, mainly in the south and other areas like in Black Wall Street, as I mentioned earlier. We will never know, but what I do know is, the time is now to try this experiment of Black unity. The other obstacle to be faced will be other groups who will try to prevent this redistribution of wealth from happening, because they will be the ones on the losing end, rather than our people for the first time. Some of the people who lose out will include people who look like you, because some Black individuals have actually worked against the betterment of their people – this is why we don't have an organization like this in place now.

Haven't you ever wondered why, with all the money, talent, and expertise our people possess, no one has put together such an organization on a national level? The last time something like this was attempted was in the 1920s. Yes, there have been groups here and there that tried building a national organization for our people, but not on this level. We've had organizations with national influence that were dealing with a specific religious group; this left many of our people out because they didn't believe in that particular religion. This organization will be about uniting our people first, in order to help them be the best they can be. Period. No alternative motives, just about helping our people live happy productive and prosperous lives.

There have been times when leaders or organizations existed that had all the qualities to bring us together, but unfortunately we relied on the individual rather than the institution, and as you know, we humans are not perfect and do make mistakes. So when the leader disgraced himself or died, so did the organization or the movement. That's why this organization has to be about more than the individual and all about the institution. The collective must always supersede the individual. We must not have one leader, but many leaders who will represent the qualities of the organization and follow through on its mission. This will ensure that if one leader falters or dies, the organization will not weaken and die, requiring us to start over again as we have had to in the past. We should learn from the past and get even stronger, letting those who are against us know they just made us that much more committed and determined to accomplish our goals. So another leader just takes his or her place. There should never be a void of true leadership like there is now.

Remember the Million Man March? Wasn't that a great accomplishment? I never felt so proud to see my brothers all together, in unity and peace, in all my life. Even though I didn't attend, I'm sure there were millions more like me who wanted to. How about the Million Woman March which was also amazing and finally the Million Family March? For all those who attended, and wanted to attend, I write this book for you. All those who came before me, who attempted or succeeded in bringing our people together in order to reach our full potential, I write this book for you. Whether it's the Million Man, Woman, or Family March, they all had one purpose in common, to support and unite of our people in order for you to reach your full potential and live a happy life.

The millions who celebrate Kwanzaa are a great example of what we can do when we have a plan and come together. Let's take this to the next level and build on those principles. This book and the organizational plan it contains are for you. We're looking for those same millions to be the first supporters of this organization, and be the example for others to follow to do the same, because you are the future leaders of our community. We're looking for five to ten million members, out of the more than forty million people in our community.

We can once again take our rightful place as masters of our own destiny and leaders with a positive influence on the world. The world watched as we came together united in a peaceful manner. Let's take the next step and show the world what we can do when we have an organization with a plan that unites us in all parts of our lives. We've done this before, and we can do it again. It's all about the program, folks. We can become a happy, healthy, and prosperous people, or we can continue to allow ourselves to be programmed by people whose only interest is in taking as much as they can from us, without giving us anything worthwhile in return. The choice is still yours.

Our minds and talents have been used to make other people prosperous; it's time we start using our minds and talents for ourselves so we can become prosperous. Now is the time to take action. We will have a group of experienced, successful members, in the fields of accounting, business, mental health, physical health, finances, technology, and education. They will help to guide us in setting up the organization, and to help us make the right choices in our lives – not some of the time, but all of the time. All we ask of you is to participate by going to the website, by getting the word out, by becoming a member, and by getting involved in all the organization has to offer. Our goal is to raise five hundred million to a billion dollars. Don't get scared. Membership is only one hundred dollars a year. You can pay monthly or annually.

You can also support us by making donations. For less than you spend on a cup of coffee a day, you can be a part of the solution to finally bringing us together and reaping the full benefits, which we've been giving to other communities since we were first brought here in chains. There's really no excuse now. Money is not the issue. You spend more on coffee, sodas, junk food, lottery tickets, partying, clothes and other kinds of products with little to no value than it will take to support this organization. Why not be a part of something great that will help not only you, but your people as well. After all, we've been building and making other communities happy and prosperous since we came to this country. Don't you think it's time we start doing the same for our community?

This organization is about giving you more than what you put in. As a member, you'll benefit from at least one of the programs or services offered, whether it's physically, mentally, spiritually, financially, or all the above. It's time to choose what you think is important to you and your people. You have nothing to lose and your mental, physical, and financial freedom to gain. This will take time, sacrifice, honesty, determination, patience and trust – are you ready?

The organization will be about providing all that has been discussed in previous chapters of this book. I'm about this. I've proven it by taking the first step in writing this book. What will you be about?

It's time to break the cycle of self-hatred and continuing the slave mind. In the past, our great leaders were killed trying to make our lives better. Our organizations were destroyed because when our leaders died, we let the movement die too. Are you going to continue to give your hard-earned money to support the same people who killed our leaders and infiltrated our organizations, while your people need help and continue to suffer?

This organization is about bringing back at least ten percent of those trillion dollars we spend every year with everyone but us. Ask yourself this most important question: Are you worth at least ten percent of what you spend? We're talking about one hundred billion dollars staying in your community to help you and your people. Challenge yourself, your family and friends, and your people – challenge me and challenge the organization to prove we can accomplish this. It will take all our efforts to do this.

As I said before, some of our people don't want to unite. It's not in their best interest or they just don't think we can do this. The people who will support and get this organization started first, are the "million march" members, both those who came and those who didn't but wanted to. These are the people who've been waiting for this since the "million marches" and even before then. They realize that something is missing in our community, that we aren't working together as a people, in order to be the best we can be, in order to reach our full potential.

The people that marched are looking for direction and leadership on how we can come together. These people will be the base upon which this foundation will be built on. They'll be the ones spreading the word about this book and the organization. If you've read this far, I'm talking about you. Change doesn't always occur at the top; most of the time, it takes everyday people to start a revolution or a movement (they call it "grassroots" now). If you look at our past, from Booker T. Washington with the Tuskegee Institute, the Honorable Marcus Garvey with the UNIA, the Honorable Elijah Muhammad with the Nation of Islam, to the Black Panthers (and the many others you haven't heard of), you will see that great things have been accomplished by people from humble beginnings. So yes, we can do this, and reach the majority of our people with not only a message of unity, but a message of creating a better life for all of us, the message of determining our own future.

Some of you skeptics and non-believers are probably saying that the organizations mentioned did not last or are not as big as they once were. Well, this is true, but I say these organizations didn't last because of reasons I mentioned earlier. We learn from those reasons, this organization will not be stopped because every single one of you, are the organization. It will not be one leader, but many leaders including you. Focusing on a figurehead, not having qualified people in place, listening to traitors in our community, and most importantly, having an institution that is not bigger than its leaders is what stopped us in the past. That's why it's important to learn from the past so you don't repeat the same mistakes in the future.

There are examples of organizations that have lasted for decades because the institution became bigger than its leaders. Can you name the President of the NAACP, UNCF, Urban League, and others? Although I think they kind of lost their way in certain areas, they still provide a need in our community. Just like how people found out about the million marches through organized committees, and word of mouth. Word of mouth is the most powerful tool in our world to getting the word out. Since we need a financial base, the membership money and donations will be used to buy the first building, where the organization will be based and located in Oakland, California (where the Black Panthers started).

The organization will start to build stores and credit unions across the country. Our opening up savings accounts will allow the credit unions to raise money to help members save money on credit card interest, using loans and balance transfers. This will allow them to have the money to give loans as said before in the financial section, and allow you to receive higher interest rates on your savings. The money would continue to recycle in our community instead of someone else's.

Right now you are saving your hard-earned money in banks that are only thinking about their bottom line, not yours. They're offering you the lowest interest possible in your savings account, while at the same time charging you the highest interest on your loans, credit cards, and monthly service fees, while doing very little in your community.

Banks receive money for the purpose of giving loans to businesses, home owners and others – but now the interest rates are so low that these banks don't feel the need to loan any money, which is part of the problem why our economy is slow in recovering. These banks borrow money at the lowest rates in history, and make money off the difference between the interest they get the money for and the interest they get from other safe investments here and around the world. But banks won't fulfill their mission to small businesses, people trying to buy homes, and other people trying to better their condition. There's something wrong with this picture – don't you think? – but our elected officials have allowed this to go on.

Unfortunately, some people may not be interested in some of the other programs the organization will offer, but I know you're interested in making and saving more money then you are now. Just by simply joining the organization and opening an account with our credit union will put billions – not millions, but billions – back into our community. This will allow us to help others in the community as well. It's just common sense to do this (although I know we don't always use common sense, it's time to change that). Remember, other than the membership fee, you're not spending any more money than you already are. You're simply redirecting it to an institution and businesses that are all about helping you and your community.

Stores will be opened up across the country, in the buildings the organization owns, that will sell items you buy every day, at a discount so you save in this area as well. This will give members another major incentive for joining. Once the financial base is in place and running well, we can start on the other departments mentioned in the other sections of the book.

We ask that you make a commitment to the organization for at least two years. If you don't see the results we promise, you've only lost less than what it would cost to drink a cup of coffee a day for two years, and of course the disappointment of not realizing the potential of all the things that an organization like this could do for our people. But you won't have to worry about that because the people who'll be working with the organization will have the dedication, commitment, patience, honesty, sacrifice, and trust it will take to make this organization the best it can be. Why? Because they're already doing this in their chosen fields. We are not trying to reinvent the wheel, but just unite us all under one umbrella.

If you do your part to support the organization, we will do ours to make sure the organization does what it's supposed to do. If you don't support this organization on some level, then you should ask yourself why, considering you haven't given serious effort to try it. You're acknowledging that you are still under the chains of mental slavery because this is worthwhile in so many ways, not only to you, but to all our people and will change our lives forever.

In my opinion, in general, the world's population is made up of three types of minds, the slave mind, (followers) the open mind, (the in-betweeners) and finally the free mind, (leaders). The slave-minded person is controlled by someone or group who uses their control for their own gains, not yours. These people make decisions for you, based on their agendas, not yours. They have so much control over you that an opportunity like this, to unite our people and build an economic foundation would scare you to the point, you would find as many excuses as possible not to support this organization, because it would go against all you've been programmed to do. So you probably won't join until you see the majority of people doing it. Then there is the open-minded person. This person isn't totally controlled by the slave mind.

They're able to use logic and common sense to weigh the pros and cons of what will be best for them, but still might hesitate because of their slave mind programming. Based on this, it will take time because they'll have to find a way to convince themselves by maybe seeing others join first, but they probably will join an organization like this because they see it will be in their best interest to do so. Last but not least is the free-minded person. These people think for themselves and know a good thing when they see it. They won't hesitate to be a part of an organization like this because they know it's worth supporting and will benefit not only themselves, but the whole community. In life we think this way.

You have the leaders, trailblazers, innovators, inventors, and trendsetters, who start and are the first to initiate things. Then you have those in-betweeners who see the benefits but will take time to evaluate the situation before supporting it. Then you have the followers who finally see the benefits because everyone else already does and don't want to be left behind. Generally speaking, this is the basic makeup of how we think. There is nothing wrong with being any of these types of people, as long as the people you're following have your best interest in mind, and that's the problem with the slave mind. The people who programmed us didn't and still don't have our best interest in mind, which is the reason we're not united now like other groups. We can no longer and should no longer rely on another group of people who have proven in the past and still today, they don't have our best interest in mind, for our happiness and well being.

My goal in writing this book and creating this organization is to get us to think freely, because we've waited too long already to do this. It's been almost a hundred years since this has been done on this scale. Our people are suffering all over the world needlessly because of the slave and colonized mind – it's time to end those mindsets. So my brothers and sisters, I ask you, what mind are you? I sincerely urge you to join the organization to see for yourself if this will work or not. I truly believe it will. I'm staking my life on it. You have very little to lose, but your freedom (physically, mentally, spiritually and financially) to gain. The only way this won't work is without you.

As I said before, this is not new, Black people. We have a problem, we have the solution, and we have a plan. For too long we have relied on other people to solve our problems. I think it is time for us to solve our own, and when we did solve our problems in the past, we were successful. Our ancestors sacrificed their lives to make our futures better; let's work together again to make their dreams come true. Brothers and sisters, we've been sitting on the sidelines for way too long, watching other groups succeed at playing the game of life. It's time to get off the sidelines and get into the game, time to use our knowledge, wisdom, experience, and talents to benefit our community. We've done this before, we can do it again. We must finally begin to heal the wounds of the psychological effects of slavery and achieve the success we are capable of – and we can! I love you, my brothers and sisters.

POWER, PEACE, ASALAAM ALAYKUM,
HOTEP, SHALOM, ASANTE

Black Unity

The Ten Guidelines of Black Unity

1. **Love** – Love your family, extended family, and community with unconditional love. Put your people first. Think about where you come from, where you're going, how to get there, and how to help your people do the same.

2. **Respect** – Respect your elders, neighbors, community and yourself with support and positive reinforcement.

3. **Sacrifice** – It will take sacrifice to accomplish your goals and the goals of our people so we can reach our full potential.

4. **Patience** – You must have patience with yourself, your family and your community. Remember: it took a long time for us to get in this position; it will also take a while for things to change.

5. **Dedication** – It takes dedication and commitment to reach your full potential and the potential of our people.

6. **Balance** – We must remember to have a balanced life, in order to be successful in all the things we aspire to do.

7. **Protection** – We must physically, mentally, and spiritually protect our families and communities from negative influences from inside and outside our communities.

8. **Support** – You should support your family, friends, neighbors, and community in all the areas that will help them be the best they can be.

9. **Faith** – Challenge yourself to have faith in one another again, in order to give ourselves a chance to build a brighter future and overcome our past doubts. Faith is overcoming your fears and doubts and stepping out of your comfort zone in order to help yourself and others.

10. **Honor** – We must honor our ancestors who gave their lives in order to make our lives better, by being more responsible for our people, and to help one another in whatever way we can.

REFERENCES

THE SOLUTION

American Health and Beauty Aids Institute –
http://ahbai.org

"Deacons for Defense (TV Movie)" Wikipedia.
28 September 2011. *http://en.wikipedia.org/wiki/
Deacons_for_Defense_(TV_movie).*

Glory Foods – *http://gloryfoods.com*

"Montgomery Bus Boycott" Wikipedia. 28 September 2011.
http://en.wikipedia.org/wiki/Montgomery_Bus_Boycott

The Vernon Johns Story. Dir. Kenneth Fink. Prod. Mitchell
Galin. Laurel Entertainment, Inc, 1994

"Will Congress Finally Fund Justice for Black Farmers?"
National Black Farmers Association. 24 March 2010.
4 October 2011. *http://www.blackfarmers.org/html/032410.
html*

"Obama Signs Measure Funding Black Farmers Settlement."
CNN Politics. Online. 8 December 2010. 4 October 2011.
*http://articles.cnn.com/2010-12-08/politics/obama.black.
farmers_1_national-black-farmers-association-minority-
farmers-glickman-case?_s=PM:POLITICS*

RE-EDUCATION

"Advertising." Wikipedia. 28 September 2011. *http://en.wikipedia.org/wiki/Advertising*

"Big Cities Battle Dismal Graduation Rates." *CBS Online.* 11 February 2009. 4 October 2011. *http://www.cbsnews.com/ stories/2008/04/01/national/main3985714.shtml*

Goetzke, Kathyrn. "How Long Does it Take for an Action to Become a Habit: 21, 28, or 66 Days?" Blog. PsychCentral. com. 4 October 2011. *http://blogs.psychcentral.com/ adhd/2010/05/how-long-does-it-take-an-action-to-become-a-habit-21-28-or-66-days/*

"Marcus Garvey and the Universal Negro Improvement Association." Web page. *National Humanities Center.* 6 October 2011. *http://nationalhumanitiescenter.org/tserve/ twenty/tkeyinfo/garvey.htm*

Newby-Clark, Ian. "Creatures of Habit: Effective Advice for Lasting Habit Change." Blog hosted on *Psychology Today Online.* 4 October 2011. *http://www.psychologytoday.com/ blog/creatures-habit*

Perner, Lars. "The Psychology of Marketing." Web page. 5 October 2011. *http://www.consumerpsychologist.com/*

"The Middle Passage." *USHistory.org.* Web page. 4 October 2011. *http://www.ushistory.org/us/6b.asp*

Woodson, Carter G. *The Mis-Education of the Negro.* Sauk Village: African American Images, 2000.

EDUCATION

Ben-Jochannan, Josef. *Africa, Mother of Western Civilization.*
Baltimore: Black Classic Press, 1997

Clark, Josh. "Did the Ancient Greeks get their Ideas from
the Africans?" Howstuffworks.com. 28 September 2011.
http://www.howstuffworks.com/greek-philosophers-african-tribes.htm

Harlem Children's Zone. *http://www.hcz.org/*

"Marva Collins." Wikipedia.21 September 2011.
http://en.wikipedia.org/wiki/Marva_Collins

"Providence St. Mel." Wikipedia. 21 September 2011.
http://en.wikipedia.org/wiki/Providence_St._Mel

Rogers, J.A. *Africa's Gift to America.* New York: Helga Rogers,
1961

"United States Jewish Education – Jewish Day Schools,
Synagogue, Education, Informal Education, Conclusion."
StateUniversity.com Education Encyclopedia. 4 October
2011. *http://education.stateuniversity.com/pages/2136/Jewish-Education-UnitedStates.html*

FAMILY

Black in America 2. News feature series. *CNN Online.* 16
July 2009. 29 September 2011. *http://www.cnn.com/SPECIALS/2009/black.in.america/*

Carson, Ben. *Gifted Hands.* Ben Carson and Cecil Murphey:
2009.

Claudine. Dir. John Berry. Prod. Dick di Bona, et al. 20th
Century Fox. 1974.

"Finding Our History: African-American Names."
FamilyEducation. 4 October 2011. *http://life.familyeducation.
com/baby/baby-names/45480.html*

Gipson, Brooklyne. "The Facts about Black Marriage." *The
Loop21.* 15 April 2009. 29 September 2011. *http://archive.
theloop21.com/news/the-facts-about-black-marriage*

Gifted Hands. Dir. Thomas Carter. Prod. Bruce Stein, et al.
Sony Pictures Home Entertainment, 2009.

Hymowitz, Kay. "The Black Family: 40 Years of Lies"
4 October 2011. *http://www.city-journal.org/html/15_3_black_
family.html*

"Marriage and Divorce: The Statistics." Web page. *drphil.com.*
6 October 2011. *http://www.drphil.com/articles/article/351*

Matze, Claire. "African Baby Names." Web page. *Babyzone.
com.* 4 October 2011. *http://www.babyzone.com/pregnancy/
babynames/article/african-baby-names–*

Nation of Islam – *http://noi.org*

"Sexual Revolution in 1960s America." Wikipedia.
28 September 2011. *http://en.wikipedia.org/wiki/
Sexual_revolution_in_1960s_America*

Stefkovich, Connie. "Should We Force Children to eat
or Reward Them for Cleaning their Plate?" *Nebraska
Department of Education.* 6 October 2011. *http://www.
education.ne.gov/NS/CACFP/Caring/cleanplate.html*

"The Clean-Your-Plate Club May Turn Children into
Overeaters." *PhysOrg.com.* 6 March 2009. 4 October 2011.
http://www.physorg.com/news155558799.html

The Pursuit of Happyness. Dir. Gabriele Muccino. Prod.
Overbrook Entertainment.

HEALTH

"African American Blood Donation." Southern Illinois University School of Medicine, Office of Public Affairs. Web page. 6 March 2007. 4 October 2011. *http://www. siumed.edu/news/Newsline%20TEXT07/3-06-07.html*

"Chitterlings." Wikipedia. 28 September 2011. *http://en.wikipedia.org/wiki/Chitterlings*

"Distrust of Health System Keeps Black Males from Getting Care." Healthfinder. Online. 10 January 2011. 14 January 2011. *http://www.healthfinder.gov/news/newsstory. aspx?docID=648807*

Levy, Jens and M. Christina Garces. "Diets of Africans." 2004. Online. Gale *Nutrition and Well-Being A to Z. http://www.encyclopedia.com/doc/1G23436200016.html*

Miss Evers Boys. Dir. Joseph Sargent. Prod. Derek Kavanaugh and Kip Konwiser. HBO, 1997.

"Statistics on Health Disparities among African Americans." NetWellness. 4 October 2011. – *http://www.netwellness.org/ healthtopics/aahealth/currentstats.cfm*

"The Tuskegee Study Timeline." Web page. 4 October 2011. *http://www.cdc.gov/tuskegee/timeline.htm*

Tubbs, Sharon. "Intestinal Fortitude." *St. Petersburg Times Online.* 27 December 2002. October 2011. *http://www. sptimes.com/2002/12/27/Floridian/Intestinal_fortitude.shtml*

"Vegetarian Diets." *American Heart Association. American Heart Association Online.* 4 October 2011. *http://www.heart.org/ HEARTORG/GettingHealthy/NutritionCenter/Vegetarian-Diets_UCM_306032_Article.jsp*

BUSINESS AND FINANCE

Anderson, Claud. *Black Labor, White Wealth*. Bethesda: PowerNomics Corporation of America, 1994

Kunjufu, Jawanza. *Black Economics*. Sauk Village: African American Images, 2002.

Robinson, Randall. *The Debt: What America Owes to Blacks*. New York: Plume, 2001.

"Should There Be Slave Reparations?" VideoWired.com Originally from CNN. 23 July 2007. 4 October 2011. *http://www.videowired.com/video/1763564669/*

Viles, Peter. "Suit Seeks Billions in Slave Reparations." CNN. 27 March 2002. 28 September 2011. *http://archives.cnn.com/2002/LAW/03/26/slavery.reparations/index.html*

Williams, Lena. "Spike Lee Says Money from Blacks Saved 'X'" New York Times. *New York Times Online*. 20 May 1992. *http://www.nytimes.com/1992/05/20/movies/spike-lee-says-money-from-blacks-saved-x.htmlres=9E0CE6DB1338F933A15 756C0A964958260*

Wilson, Jay Jay and Ron Wallace. *Black Wallstreet*. Queens: Seaburn Publishing, 2008.

"What Happened to Black Wall Street on June 1, 1921?" *San Francisco BayView Newspaper Online*. 9 February 2011. 4 October 2011. *http://sfbayview.com/2011/what-happened-to-black-wall-street-on-june-1-1921/*

THE PROBLEM

A Girl like Me. Documentary. Dir. Kiri Davis. Prod. Kiri Davis. Reel Works Teen Filmmaking, 2005.

"African- American Soldiers in the Civil War." *History.com.* Web page. 4 October 2011. *http://www.history.com/topics/ african-american-soldiers-in-the-civil-war*

Akbar, Na'im. *Breaking the Chains of Psychological Slavery.* Tallahassee: Mind Productions & Associates, 1996

"Annual Report on the Federal Workforce, Fiscal Year 2008: Composition of Federal Workforce." U.S. Equal Employment Opportunity Commission. 4 October 2011 *http://www.eeoc.gov/federal/reports/fsp2008/index.html*

"Black Codes." Wikipedia. 28 September 2011. *http://en.wikipedia.org/wiki/Black_Codes_(United_States)*

Black Magic: The History of Blacks in College and Professional Basketball. Dir. Dan Klores. Prod. ESPN Films. ESPN. October 28, 2008.

Clark, Kenneth and Mamie Clark. "Racial Identification and Preferences in Negro Children." 1940-41. CNN. 29 September 2011. *http://i2.cdn.turner.com/cnn/2010/ images/05/13/doll.study.1947.pdf*

"Disfranchisement after the Reconstruction Era." Wikipedia. 29 September 2011. *http://en.wikipedia.org/wiki/ Disfranchisement_after_Reconstruction_era_(United_States)*

Fosty, George Robert. *Black Ice – The Lost History of the Colored Hockey League of the Maritimes – 1895-1925.* Halifax: Nimbus Pub Ltd, 2003

Frazier, E. Franklin. *The Negro Family in the United States.* Notre Dame: University of Notre Dame Press, 2000.

"Freedman." Wikipedia. 28 September 2011. *http://en.wikipedia.org/wiki/Freedmen*

"Freedman's Bureau." Wikipedia. 28 September 2011. *http://en.wikipedia.org/wiki/Freedmen%27s_Bureau*

Givhan, Robin. "Oprah and the View From Outside Hermes' Paris Door." *The Washington Post.* The Washington Post Online. 24 June 2005. 5 October 2011. *http://www.washingtonpost.com/wp-dyn/content/article/2005/06/23/AR2005062302086.html*

Graham, Laurence Otis. *Our Kind of People: Inside America's Black Upper Class.* New York: Harper Perennial, 1999

"Incarceration in the United States." Wikipedia. 28 September 2011. *http://en.wikipedia.org/wiki/Incarceration_in_the_United_States*

Isidore, Chris. "Nothing But Net: Basketball Dollars by School." Online. CNN Money. 18 March 2010. 4 October 2011. *http://money.cnn.com/2010/03/18/news/companies/basketball_profits/index.htm*

Johnson, Roy S. "The Jordan Effect." New York: Fortune, 1998. Online. CNN Money. 21 September 2011. *http://money.cnn.com/magazines/fortune/fortune_archive/1998/06/22/244166/index.htm*

Justice. Dir. Jeanne-Marie Almonor and John Shulman. Prod. Jeanne-Marie Shulman, et al. Image Entertainment, 2004.

Kindles, Coby. "Goal of Recycling Black spending Still a Distant Dream." *The Louisiana Weekly Online.* 11 May 2011. 21 September 2011. *http://www.louisianaweekly.com/goal-of-recycling-black-spending-still-a-distant-dream/*

"Kiri Davis." Wikipedia. 29 September 2010. *http://en.wikipedia.org/wiki/Kiri_Davis*

"Lebron and Childhood Friends Launch LRMR Marketing Company." *Current.* Online. 27 September 2008. 4 October 2011. *http://m.current.com/sports/89346311_lebron-and-childhood-friends-launch-lrmr- sports-marketing-company.htm*

Lynch, Willie. "The Willie Lynch Letter." African
    American Images. Online. 4 October 2011. *http://www.
    africanamericanimages.com/aai/willie%20lynch.htm*

Malcolm X – Make it Plain. Dir. Orlando Bagwell. Prod. Denise
    Greene, et al. Mpi Home Video, 1997

"Michael Jackson's Health and Appearance." Wikipedia.
    28 September 2011. *http://en.wikipedia.org/wiki/
    Michael_Jackson%27s_health_and_appearance*

Moore, John R. "Black History: Introduction." Web page. 4
    October 2011. *http://blackhistoryjohnmoore.bravehost.com*

Nelson, Sophia A. "The Real Affirmative Action Babies."
    The Root. 3 August 2009. 28 September 2011. *http://www.
    theroot.com/views/real-affirmative-action-babies*

"On Denny's Menu: Discrimination." *The New York Times.*
    New York Times Online. 27 May 1994. 4 October 2011.
    *http://www.nytimes.com/1994/05/27/opinion/on-denny-s-
    menu-discrimination.html*

*On the Shoulders of Giants: The Story of the Greatest Team You
    Never Heard Of.* Dir. Deborah Morales. Prod. Kareem
    Abdul Jabbar, et al. Union Productions, 2011.

"Prison Industrial Complex." Wikipedia. 28 September 2011.
    http://en.wikipedia.org/wiki/Prison_industrial_complex

Reconstruction: A State Divided. Web site. 29 September 2011.
    http://lsm.crt.state.la.us/cabildo/cab11.htm

"Redlining." Wikipedia. 28 September 2011.
    http://en.wikipedia.org/wiki/Redlining

Roth, Zachary. "Help Wanted – Sixty-five Million Need Not
    Apply." Yahoo News. 23 March 2011. 28 September 2011.
    *http://news.yahoo.com/s/yblog_thelookout/20110323/ts_yblog_
    thelookout/help-wanted-sixty-five-million-need-not-apply*

Rudulph, Elizabeth, and Harriet Barovick. "Driving While
    Black." *Time Magazine.* 15 June 1998. Accessed from Time.
    com. 4 October 2011. *http://www.time.com/time/magazine/*
    article/0,9171,988558,00.html

School Daze. Dir. Spike Lee. Prod. Spike Lee, et al. Sony
    Pictures Home Entertainment, 1998

Seeman, Jeffrey. "An Alternative View on Affirmative
    Action." Copyright 1995. 28 September 2011. *http://*
    uwacadweb.uwyo.edu/AshleyWY/affirmative_action.htm

Slavery and the Making of America. Dir. Dante J. James. Prod.
    Dante J. James. PBS, 2004. *http://www.pbs.org/wnet/slavery/*
    about/index.html

Street, Paul. "Race, Prison, and Poverty – The Race to
    Incarcerate in the Age of Correctional Keynesianism."
    Z Magazine, May 2001. Accessed from Thirdworldtraveler.
    com. 4 October 2011. *http://www.thirdworldtraveler.com/*
    Prison_System/Race_Prison_Poverty.html

"Study: White and Black Children Biased Towards Lighter
    Skin." Article and video. *Anderson Cooper 360.* CNN. 14
    May 2010. 29 September 2011. *http://www.cnn.com/2010/*
    US/05/13/doll.study/index.html

Thompson, Krissah. "Harvard Professor Arrested at Home."
    Washington Post Online. 21 July 2009. 29 September
    2011. *http://www.washingtonpost.com/wp-dyn/content/*
    article/2009/07/20/AR2009072001358.html

The Civil War. Dir. Kenneth Lauren Burns. Prod. American
    Documentaries, Inc., et al. PBS (DIRECT), 1990.

"The Ever-Changing Face of Michael Jackson." *New York Daily*
    News Online. Photo feature. 26 June 2009. 4 October 2011.
    http://www.nydailynews.com/entertainment/michael_jackson/
    *galleries/the_many_facesof_michael_jackson/the_many_faces_*
    of_michael_jackson.htm

Uneven Fairways: The Story of the Negro Leagues of Golf. Dir. Dan
    Levinson. Prod. Keith Allo, et al. Moxie Pictures, 2009.

White, Jack E. "Texaco's White-Collar Bigots." *Time
    Magazine.* Time Magazine Online. 18 November 1996.
    4 October 2011. *http://www.time.com/time/magazine/
    article/0,9171,985551,00.html*

"What is White Flight?" *WiseGeek.* Web page. 4 October 2011.
    http://www.wisegeek.com/what-is-white-flight.htm

"Whites Only Scholarship at Black College, Alabama State,
    Stirs Controversy." *FindArticles.* 11 October 1999. 4 October
    2011. *http://findarticles.com/p/articles/mi_m1355/is_19_96/
    ai_57042470/*

Williams, Walter E. "Diversity Disparities Racist, Except in
    Sports." *Orange County Register Online.* OCRegister.com.
    28 January 2011. 21 September 2011. *http://articles.ocregister.
    com/2010-01-28/opinion/24625292_1_diversity-and-inclusion-
    diversity-disparities-gender-report-card*

X, Malcolm and Alex Haley. *The Autobiography of Malcolm X.*
    Mattituck: Ameroen Ltd., 2008.

A PERSONAL MESSAGE TO MY BROTHERS AND SISTERS IN AFRICA

"Colonisation of Africa." Wikipedia. 28 September 2011. *http://
    en.wikipedia.org/wiki/Colonization_of_Africa*

"Scramble for Africa." Wikipedia. 28 September 2011.
    http://en.wikipedia.org/wiki/Scramble_for_Africa

Mutume, Gumisai. "Whither the Debt?" – Africa Recovery,
    Vol. 15, No.3 October 2001. pg.26. Accessed from UN.Org.
    4 October 2011. *http://www.un.org/ecosocdev/geninfo/afrec/
    vol15no3/153debt.htm*

"Debt Relief under the Heavily Indebted Poor Countries (HIPC) Initiative." Factsheet. *International Monetary Fund.* Online. 16 December 2010. 4 October 2011. *http://www.imf. org/external/np/exr/facts/hipc.htm*

CONCLUSION

Austin, Algernon. "What a Recession Means for Black America." Economic Policy Institute. 18 January 2008. 28 September 2011. *http://www.epi.org/publication/ib241/*

"Bailout is a Windfall to Banks, if Not to Borrowers." *New York Times Online.* 17 January 2009. 4 October 2011. *http://www.nytimes.com/2009/01/18/business/18bank. html?pagewanted=all*

"Banks Leaving Poor Neighborhoods, Expanding in Rich Ones." The Loop21 Archive. Online. 23 February 2011. 4 October 2011. *http://archive.theloop21.com/news/ banks-leaving-poor-neighborhoods-expanding-rich-ones*

Kimberley, Margaret. "Freedom Rider: A Whiter New York City." *Blackagendareport.com.* Online. 2 February 2011. 28 September 2011. *http://blackagendareport.com/search/ node/A%20Whiter%20New%20York%20City*

Patterson, Orlando. "For African Americans, A Virtual Depression – Why?" *The Nation.* The Nation Online.19 July 2010. 28 September 2011. *http://thenation.com/article/36882*

"Vanishing Chocolate Cities: The Failure of the Black Middleclass." *The FreshXpress.* Online. 26 December 2010. 4 October 2011. *http://thefreshxpress.com/2010/12/ vanishing-chocolate-cities-the-failure-of-the-black-middle-class/*

www.ingramcontent.com/pod-product-compliance
Lightning Source LLC
Chambersburg PA
CBHW072125090426
42739CB00012B/3069